DANGEROUS NARRATIVES

*An inside look into
'the mind-forged manacles'
of the Muslim world*

Muhanad Halvani

To my mother, Esma, and my father, Sami.

For your unconditional love and support—it is impossible to thank you adequately for everything you've done. I could not have asked for better parents or role models.

I wander through each chartered street,

Near where the chartered Thames does flow;

A mark in every face I meet,

Marks of weakness, marks of woe.

In every cry of every man,

In every infant's cry of fear,

In every voice, in every ban,

The mind-forged manacles I hear.

~ William Blake ~

Contents

Acknowledgments

First of all, I would like to thank God. If it weren't for his patience, mercy, and providence, I certainly wouldn't have been able to write this book, and I would be in a darker place today.

Moving on to the mortals on this list, my gratitude goes to:

Ahmad, by far the smarter of the Halvani brothers. If there's any logical error in this book, it's probably an instance in which I stubbornly chose to ignore his advice.

Rubina, my sister-in-law, for her comments on the introduction that prompted me to rewrite half of it.

Rebecca Zaccaria, my dear friend, for her valuable feedback, including her objections to my colorful choice of words in Chapter 13—and for our many conversations, which I always thoroughly enjoy.

Akın Sarı, my encyclopedic friend and colleague, for his insights and ideas.

Finally, I owe a special debt of gratitude to my beautiful wife, Merve, who is the most amazing person I've ever met. Her presence in my life imbued me with the mental fortitude needed to write this book.

Introduction

The old song goes, "fifty million Frenchmen can't be wrong." But what happens when fifty million Frenchmen *are* wrong. How does that change France? How does that change Frenchmen?

Mark Twain once said, "It's not what we don't know that gets us in trouble. It's what we know for sure that just ain't so." Now imagine magnifying that statement in scale to encompass not one, not fifty million, but almost two billion people? What happens when a quarter of the world's population clings to beliefs and narratives that "just ain't so?"

The impact of these distorted narratives on the people who hold them depends on the nature of the said narratives. Narratives that deal with trifles are of trifling consequence. On the other hand, narratives that determine how we see ourselves and our world are the *Roi Soleil* in the Versailles of the mind.

Søren Kierkegaard believed that our lives are determined by our actions, which, in turn, are determined by our choices. Therefore, how we make those choices is critical.[1] In this process, the narratives we uphold are a key element. So, when they go awry, they cast a shadow over everything, malforming the lives of those who hold onto them and the world they live in.

The current troubles in Muslim countries do not arise from the vagaries of fate but the sins of man. In particular, they reflect the *dangerous narratives* that Muslims uphold. In this book, I provide insights into what these narratives are.

Now, you may be wondering what qualifies me to write about Muslims. There are, after all, a plethora of self-proclaimed experts on Muslims these days.

I am a Muslim born and raised. I have been privy to the comedy of errors in the Muslim world since the day I was born. The narratives that I identify are not polemics divorced from reality. They are not drawn from a Gallup poll, or a verse in an ancient text. They are drawn from my life. I have encountered them repeatedly – in dining-room discussions, during Friday sermons at the mosque, and in the lecture halls of the university where I teach. I have seen how these narratives have bled into the social and political fabric of my homeland – and how they shape this part of the world. This book was born out of my frustration in trying to figure out why things are the way they are and how things can be changed.

Furthermore, my disposition was always one of an outsider. Most people, in their efforts to fit in, internalize the scripts of the culture they are born into. However, unlike my peers, I never put much stock into fitting in when it came at the cost of intellectual independence. This is why I am able to see the problems or issues with what others take at face value.

Finally, my Muslim in-group membership provides me with an *aegis* against identity politics. It affords me the opportunity to critique Muslim culture directly without mincing words. On occasion, I do so at my own expense, for my own views have evolved over time. Some of the beliefs I criticize in this book are, to my chagrin, ones that I once held true.

But before I go on, here is a *caveat lector*.

This is not another frothing-at-the-mouth diatribe against Islam and its adherents. If that is what you seek, if you are expecting me to sink a blade into Islam like a two-bit anti-Muslim matador, then this is not the book for you. This will not reconfirm what you know – or what you think you know – about Muslims. There are plenty of books of that sort, peddling in that particular prejudice *du jour*.

In fact, one of the reasons I am writing this book is to point out the real *dangerous narratives* in the Muslim world, as opposed to the oft-cited invectives hurled against it.

Case-in-point: female circumcision or female genital mutilation (FGM). This horrible practice is often associated with Muslims. If you listen to Somali-born former Dutch parliamentarian Ayaan Hirsi Ali, you would think that FGM is a uniquely Islamic problem. Yet when we compare that narrative against a UNICEF map of FGM across Africa, we see something interesting.[2]

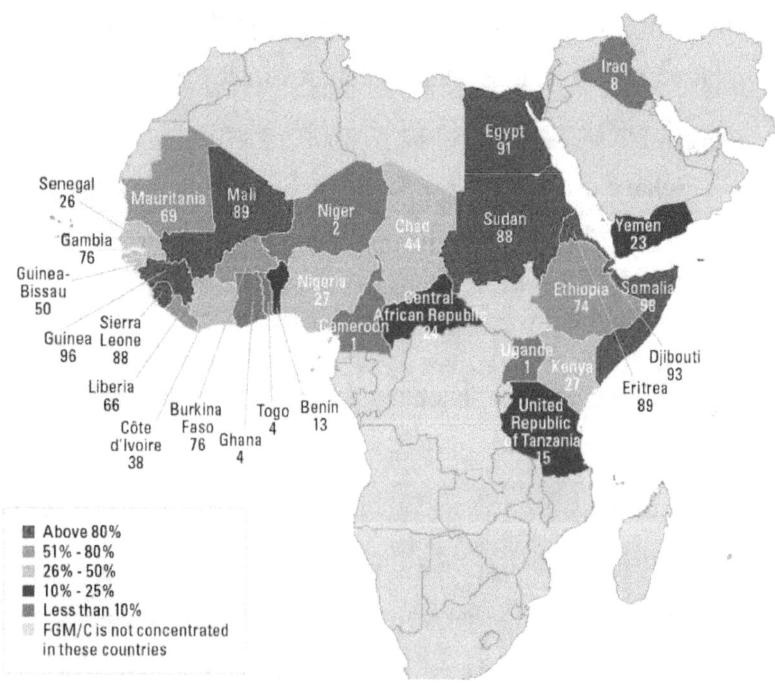

As the map illustrates, FGM is most prevalent in central African countries, where it is practiced by both Muslims *and* Christians.[3] That is because it is rooted in African cultural traditions that predate Islam, Christianity, and even recorded history.[4] It is *not* based on any religious text. As Dr. John Esposito, professor of Islamic studies at Georgetown University, states: "Female circumcision is neither an Islamic practice nor widespread among Muslims."[5] This explains why, barring a few exceptions, female circumcision is almost nonexistent in the heartland of Islam, while in Egypt – the singular Middle Eastern country in which FGM is widespread – it is practiced in spite of vehement opposition from mainstream religious authorities in that country.[6]

Another concept that polemicists have recently latched onto is *taqiyya*. This is supposedly a *carte blanche* for Muslims to lie in order to propagate their religion. So, whenever a Muslim person says anything reasonable or liberal, he is accused by the anti-Muslim crowd of practicing *taqiyya*.

The thing is, *taqiyya*, as the aforementioned anti-Muslim crowd interprets it, can only work for a non-proselytizing religion or cult. Islam, however, seeks to bring nonbelievers into its fold. It cannot condone misrepresenting itself, because then if people converted they would not be converting to Islam but a misrepresentation of it. For a religion that places so much value on dogmatic purity, that is a no-no.

Taqiyya is a permission to lie under extreme coercion, an injunction that came down when early Muslims were being tortured in the streets of Mecca just for professing their belief in the new faith. Incidentally, Albanian Muslims who hid Jewish families in their cellars during the Holocaust[7] and lied to the SS officers who came banging on their front doors looking for them were in fact practicing *taqiyya*.[a]

Then there is the lurid story of the "seventy-two virgins." Supposedly, Muslims believe that if one dies a martyr, he gets seventy-two virgins in heaven. Polemicists base their assumption that this is a widespread belief on the existence of a *hadith*[b] claiming so. While this story does indeed exist in *hadith* compilations, it is deemed weak or

---

[a] Ever pragmatic, Islam also condones lying to your wife if she ever asks you, "Do I look fat in this dress?" Regardless of the truth, the *halal* answer is always "No."

[b] *Hadith* are the written accounts of the actions and sayings of the Prophet Muhammad that were compiled around two hundred years after his death through a long chain of oral transmitters. It is important to remember that not all *hadiths* are seen as equal. Some are deemed authentic, others are deemed weak, and some are deemed to be fabrications.

inauthentic and hence has no traction in Muslim society. In fact, most Muslims, myself included, had not even heard of it until it was avidly seized upon by a coterie of right-wing media outlets.

These are not the only examples. Nowadays, popular discourse on Muslims is not concerned with honest intellectual inquiry, nor does it seek to develop a genuine understanding of Muslim societies. It is solely concerned with "proving" predetermined conclusions in support of particular political agendas. Hence the methodology of many anti-Muslim polemicists consists mainly of rummaging through the Quran and *Hadith* for verses and stories high on shock value in order to build their case that Islam – and, by extension, its adherents – are evil. Usually, though, what they dig up is either taken out of context, or comprised of obscure, unsubstantiated *hadiths* to which no one in mainstream Muslim society gives credence. Their methodology is akin to someone trying to understand Jews and Christians on the basis of what is written in the Old Testament alone. Whilst those writers provide their target audience with the soothing reassurance that comes with confirmation bias, they leave them with no genuine understanding of the Muslim world.

This book does not regurgitate the *de rigeur* allegations against Islam and Muslims, nor is it another *Muslims Are All Awesome, Kumbayah Edition.* This is not an anodyne human-interest fluff piece on the multicultural idiosyncrasies in a Muslim family. You will not find funny stories about a spunky teenage hijabi girl and her shenanigans that make you feel all warm and fuzzy and reaffirm your belief in humanity.

In fact, I anticipate many Muslims will be upset that this book is too critical and negative, that it does not examine all the admirable qualities in Muslim culture.

It is true. This book is not a comprehensive overview of the Muslim mind. If you are looking to understand how Muslims think in general day-to-day life, then I highly recommend Dr. Margaret K. Nydell's book *Understanding Arabs*, which is one of the fairest accounts I have found on the subject.[a]

This book is instead a Conradian journey into the Muslim mind from someone who knows the lay of the

---

[a] For a long time the definitive book on the subject was *The Arab Mind* by Raphael Patai. Though well-written and insightful, it is also extremely outdated as it was published in 1972 and has not been updated much since then. If you're not already knowledgeable about Arab culture, and able to distinguish information that is still applicable from that which is not, I would not recommend that book.

mental landscape. It does not seek to fully represent Muslims but rather shed light on the mental demons that torment them and hold them back.

Muslim societies are in dire straits: politically, economically, and socially. Politically, the Muslim world is a shabby string of failed states, dictatorships, and oligarchies. According to the annual Freedom in the World report conducted by the nonpartisan organization Freedom House, eleven out of the twenty least free countries in the world are Muslim-majority states. Not even one country in the entire Muslim world from the Persian Gulf to the Atlantic was ranked as "Free."[8]

Economically, the Muslim world is not better off. Muslims comprise nearly a quarter of the world's population yet contribute only 8 percent of the world's GDP,[9] 1.6 percent of the world's patents, and 6 percent of the world's academic publications.[10] The number of scientists, engineers, and technicians *per capita* in Muslim countries is 20 percent of the world average. These facts are unsurprising given that nearly 40 percent of the Muslim world's population is illiterate.[11]

Even socially, the area about which Muslims are most confident, the trends are disconcerting. According to a major study conducted at the University of Washington, suicide, murder, rape, and mental health conditions are all skyrocketing in Muslim-majority countries.[12]

Overall, were it not for sub-Saharan Africa, the Muslim world would be at the bottom of the scale in almost every category of human development.

This book seeks to determine why the Muslim world has fallen low based on my observations and experiences. In doing so, it will posit counter-narratives that many Muslims in traditional circles might consider controversial, offensive, and maybe even treasonous. That is to be expected, for it is the classic knee-jerk reaction to any idea that storms the ramparts of the prevailing narrative.

But when the state of affairs is in such a sorry state, causing offense through iconoclastic views is not a concern but a duty. When Moses saw the Israelites worshiping the golden calf, he did not shrug it off; he burned the idol and ground it to dust. When Jesus witnessed the corrupt practices of the moneylenders in the temple in Jerusalem, he did not just walk past their stands. He overturned their tables and drove them out of that sacred site. When Muhammad received his divine revelation, he did not leave the polytheists to their false idols and barbaric ways. He fought until all the false gods in Mecca were struck down.

I do not bring up these examples in a vain attempt to place myself in the same company as humanity's finest. I do so merely to make a point: if one wants to express the truth and bring about change, one cannot blindly tow the cultural line and kowtow to the status quo. One must be willing to uphold views that some will inevitably consider deeply offensive.

That is why Socrates used to describe himself as the "gadfly" of the Athenian people. He questioned assumptions, he provoked – not as an end in itself, but to stir his fellow citizens into reexamining their cherished beliefs. In that vein, I will discuss the *dangerous narratives* in the Muslim world. And yes, just like Socrates, I do intend to sting.

A Clarification:

What is the "Muslim World"?

In the Introduction, I have used the phrase "the Muslim world" often. But what do I mean by that exactly?

It is a fair question. After all, Islam is the second-largest religion after Christianity. According to the Pew Research Center, as of 2015 there are 1.8 billion Muslims around the world – a quarter of the world's population.[13]

Most of these Muslims are not from Arab nations. In fact, only 20 percent of Muslims live in the Middle East and North Africa.[14] Of the countries with the top ten largest Muslim populations, only Egypt, which comes in fifth on the list, is in the Middle East.[15] Yet in this book, I place particular emphasis on the Arab Muslim world. Most of the examples I give in this book are from the Middle East.

I do not talk about Muslim countries in Southeast Asia, where the majority of Muslims actually reside because I think what goes on in the Arab Muslim world nowadays will have a greater impact on the world stage than anything taking place in Indonesia, Malaysia, or Bangladesh. There are several reasons for this. First of all, the entire Middle East is a tinder box. There are multiple active conflicts in this region. Syria, Iraq, Yemen, and Libya are all failed states embroiled in civil wars. Lebanon, Egypt, Algeria, and Jordan are rife with social, economic, and political unrest. There is no end in sight to the Palestinian crisis. Saudi Arabia and its allies are at odds with Qatar and are threatening to develop nuclear weapons should Iran develop them as well.[16] The Kurds in Iraq, Syria, and Turkey have heavily armed militias and separatist ambitions. The Sunni-Shia rhetoric grows more acrimonious and divisive with each passing day. And in the middle of it all, we have ISIS, a group that has shown the world that, contrary to what Obi-Wan Kenobi once claimed, one can indeed find a more wretched hive of scum and villainy than Mos Eisley.

In 1888, almost a quarter-century before the start of World War I, the great German statesman Otto von Bismarck made a prescient statement: "One day the great European War will come out of some damned foolish thing in the Balkans."[17] If he were alive today, he would make the same statement about the Middle East. It is quite possible that the situation in one of these flashpoints could escalate into something much worse, especially in places like Syria, where major foreign powers are jostling against each other in support of different factions in that conflict.

In such a volatile environment, it is prudent to analyze and understand how people really think. How people perceive the world determines how they shape it, and thus, if you want to shape the world – or nudge it one way or another – you have to understand first how people perceive it. An invasion, a coup, or an "Arab Spring" cannot steer the Middle East off the catastrophic path it is on. It has to start with a brutally honest exercise of introspection.

The second reason to focus on Arab Muslims is the massive influx of "refugees" and migrants from the Middle East into Europe in the last few years. The number of these refugees is so significant that their mindset will have a profound impact on the social cohesion in that continent over the coming decades. Now, unlike the rhetoric coming from right-wing partisans and those who are aligned with them on this issue, I am not saying that the impact is predetermined to be negative. I am also not saying that they have to become carbon copies of Europeans and shed everything that defines who they are for the impact to be positive. But they will have to break free from the cultural-ghetto mentality and ditch the *dangerous narratives* that I cover in this book. Otherwise they will find no prosperity in Europe. Instead they will be consigned to a future of marginalization, disenfranchisement, embitterment, and resentment in which they will become a catalyst for turmoil and civil strife.

Finally, the Arab Muslim world has been successful in exporting its own narratives to the rest of the Muslim world. Whether due to the prevalence of Saudi-funded mosques or because this region was the cradle of Islam and contains its three holiest cities, the religio-cultural influence of the Arab Muslim world on its non-Arab coreligionists has always been disproportionately one-way. The religious discourse taking place in Malaysia, for instance, has no discernible influence on Muslims globally. The same, however, cannot be said of Saudi Arabia, which has managed between 1982 and 2005 to establish 200 Islamic colleges, 210 Islamic centers, 1,500 mosques, and 2,000 schools around the world to impose its baleful worldview.[18] So while not everything in this book will be applicable to all Muslims, many of the narratives discussed in this book are prevalent in non-Arab Muslim societies and communities as well.

With that point clarified, it is time to embark on a journey into the dark corners of the Muslim mind and uncover some *dangerous narratives*.

Chapter 1

Woe is Me: I am More Oppressed than Thou

The first narrative we are going to explore is self-victimization and the learned helplessness that goes along with it. However, to understand how this narrative came to be and how it has taken root, we have to take a step back and look at the origin story of the modern Middle East.

The seminal event that led to the formation of the modern Middle East, as we know it, was World War I. There were three events that happened during and after that war, which shaped this region. All three events are known to every child who went to school in the Middle East.

The first is the treaty of Sykes-Picot signed in 1916 between Britain and France. In it, those two countries laid out how to carve up the Ottoman Empire – including its

Arab provinces – among themselves after the war. Britain and France had previously promised Arabs their independence in exchange for rebelling against the Ottoman Turks, but neither the British nor the French intended to go through with that promise. In short, the Arabs rebelled, the Entente Powers reneged, and political unity in the Middle East was shattered in accordance with the articles of Sykes-Picot.[19]

The second event is the Balfour Declaration. This was a promise issued by the British government in 1917 to Lord Rothschild to establish and facilitate in Palestine a "national home for the Jewish People."[20] Unlike the promises that Britain made to the Arabs, this promise was actually honored. Jews from around the world were encouraged to move to Palestine and were offered both financial and military assistance while the local Arabs were repressed. This served to further destabilize the region and break the relative harmony between Muslims and Jews that had been the norm for more than a thousand years.

The third event was the combined result of the Balfour Declaration and the subsequent policies of the British Mandate that stemmed from it over the course of three decades. It had such an enormous impact on the collective memory of Muslims that to this day, it is called *al-Nakba* (The Catastrophe). This refers to the expulsion of more than 700,000 Palestinian Arabs from their homes at the hands of Jewish Zionist paramilitary militias and the formation of the State of Israel.

In all three events, Muslims play the role of victims. The tyranny of the military dictatorships that proliferated in the region following the withdrawal of the colonial powers only served to underscore that point.

Arab Muslims cannot even draw a sense of empowerment from the time they were a part of the Ottoman Empire, because their view of that period has been twisted by revisionist nationalist propaganda seeking to glorify the genesis of Arab states by depicting the preceding period as a dark age. Across the Arab world, schoolchildren are obliged to view Ottoman administration as an oppressive colonialist regime – even though up until the twentieth century it was not viewed as such in any Muslim province of the empire.[21]

So Arab Muslims not only see themselves as victims, their view of the last seven hundred years, from the time Baghdad was brutally sacked by the Mongols, reaffirms that *dangerous narrative.*

In his book, *True Believer*, philosopher Eric Hoffer notes that "there is in us a tendency to locate the shaping forces of our existence outside ourselves." We attribute success and failure to "the state of things around us."[22] A narrative of personal victimhood accentuates that tendency to a pathological level.

That is why the average person on the streets of Beirut, Cairo, Amman, or Riyadh will always lay the blame far from home. If asked why the Muslim world is in such a wretched state, he never lays the blame on his own doorstep. The blame is always pinned on a hegemonic and tyrannical "other."

To Muslims, we are in a dismal state because of American Imperialism, because of Zionists, because of our perfidious politicians. Thomas Hobbes saw the world as all-against-all; Muslims today see the world as all-against-us where everyone else is driven by a deep-seated hatred of Islam. In that equation, ordinary Muslims play no proactive role. They are just passive victims.

This situation has been exacerbated by the emergence of a recent social theory called the Theory of Intersectionality, which posits that every individual lives at the intersection of many dimensions of power. Proponents of this theory peg every race, religion, gender, and sexual orientation as well as a myriad of other classifications into a pyramid of perceived power and privilege. The theory implicitly ascribes greater moral authority the lower you are on the hierarchy.

Though many have not heard of the theory per se, its impact is unmistakable on the climate of thought. From talk shows to college campuses and politics, weakness and personal tragedy are now extolled. Every college kid wants to demonstrate that they have faced adversity; every politician claims they were born in a working class family. Whereas previous generations would shrug off the hardships in their lives, people now are encouraged to dwell on them – to capitalize on them even. It is no longer noble to transcend a life that is poor, nasty, brutish, and short; the new goal is to wallow in it.

This has not been happening just at an individual level. It has been happening at a group level as well. Every community, defined reductively according to gonads, melanin level, sexual orientation, religious affiliation, or what have you, wants to be recognized as the most oppressed, garner the most sympathy, and lay claim to the implicit virtue that comes with the deprivation of status.

Muslims, like so many others, have been lured into this ludicrous rat race. For example, it has become an increasing trend to share images of downtrodden Muslims they come across on social media. In those pictures, Muslims are either bloodied, crying, fearful, or dismembered – whichever it is, they are always in a pitiable condition, always victims.

Some of the Muslims who share these pictures say they do so to inform the world and prick its conscience into action. That is a bit rich coming from us, we who are so quick to condemn the world as morally bankrupt. Nonetheless, if we insist on playing the damsel in distress and want the world to save us, then incessantly sharing graphic images of Muslims in agony is not the way to go about it. Doing so does not rally people to our cause – it desensitizes them to our suffering.

Others claim that sharing these pictures is a show of solidarity. A noble sentiment if this is indeed the purpose, but misguided. Searing our collective memory with defeatist imagery is actually detrimental to in-group cohesion. Naturally, people do not want to be associated with the losing side. When Muslims constantly portray themselves as poor, pitiable creatures, many Muslims will stop identifying as Muslims. And are they to blame? Who wants to be part of a group that is constantly down on their luck.

And worst of all, these image reinforce the *dangerous narrative* that we are victims. This in turn robs us of our agency.

Nothing robs a man of the ability to change his lot, like the self-infantilizing notion of victimhood. I use the term infantilizing because when a person self-classifies as a victim, their locus of control shifts from an internal one to an external one. In other words, they disempower themselves; they forfeit their ability to change their lot. Thus a person stops being an adult and becomes a mere simulacrum of an adult.

To make matters worse, those who self-identify as "victims" eventually do suffer, as their imagination brings reality in line with itself. The label they ascribe themselves turns into a self-fulfilling prophecy. How can people in this region ever thrive if they keep perceiving themselves as victims?

I once came across a picture that I will never forget. The picture was taken during the First World War on the Western Front. It shows a couple standing in front of their home which lay completely in ruins. Nothing remains of the house, except the basement, where the couple live. What is most fascinating about this picture is that the couple are smartly dressed – the man in a suit and his wife in a dress. They stand upright, their pose betraying none of the tragedy in their lives. If it were not for the background, the picture might well have been taken at a wedding or an evening ball.

Seeing that picture, I am not surprised that Europe survived two of the most devastating wars the world has ever seen and rose from the ashes the way it did. People who stand proud in the face of tragedy will overcome it. Those who weep and lament, the way Muslims have been doing over the past hundred years, will be overwhelmed by it.

Look how the Nazis sought to overcome the legacy of Germany's defeat in the First World War and their humiliation in the Treaty of Versailles. Their crimes aside, the Nazis had a firm grasp on human psychology. They understood, as Eric Hoffer pointed out, that those who seek to transform a nation cannot do so by breeding discontent. Instead they must "kindle and fan an extravagant hope."[23]

The imagery they conveyed in their rallies, spectacles, and propaganda material like the documentary *Triumph of the Will* all served that purpose. They were consciously designed to restore the pride of a broken people, to make them believe in themselves again.

And they achieved that goal. How they later put that renewed vitality into practice is beside the point. It does not diminish from the fact that their approach to galvanizing the nation worked.

If Muslims are to transcend their circumstances, they need to reclaim their sense of agency. As British activist Maajid Nawaz argues, Muslims need to start acting "in a positive and empowering way, instead of constantly playing the victim card" and embrace a "post-victimization" narrative where past grievances take a back seat to participation, contribution, and development.[24]

As for the hardships Muslims endure, they are what they are. The Buddha explained it in a philosophical concept called the Dukkha. Shakespeare expressed it in a more poetic way when he said, "The flesh is heir to a thousand natural shocks." Dr. Jordan Peterson, professor of psychology at the University of Toronto calls it "the burden of being."[25] Whichever way you choose to put it, it all boils down to the same thing: "Life is suffering."

Muslims have a choice. They can either shoulder the burden of being and by doing so mitigate their suffering.

Or they can stay tethered to a metaphorical Wailing Wall, carry on living as imploding beanbags of self-pity, and see their burden compounded.

Marcus Aurelius once said, "Be the stone cliff against which the waves constantly break, standing firm against the fury of the sea." That is how Muslims need to approach life and being. Unfortunately, so far there is little indication that such a perceptive shift is taking place in the Muslim community. Instead Muslims seem determined to go down the road, nay the cul-de-sac, of self-pity.

Chapter 2

Scotland will be Free when Scotsmen become *True* Scotsmen

As we saw in the previous chapter, Muslims are always ready to blame others for their woes. So aren't there Muslims who point at themselves as the source of the present state of affairs?

Indeed there are but the argument is itself a *dangerous narrative.*

A common view in the Muslim world, especially among the religiously inclined, is that Muslims have abandoned their faith. They are not observant enough. That is why the Muslim world is in such a sorry state. They assert that Muslims in the past were pious, godly, righteous men... *true* Muslims. Only when Muslims become true Muslims again will they relive the glories of ages past.

This narrative comes with its own canards. The story goes that David Ben-Gurion, national founder and first prime minister of Israel, proclaimed that when mosques are as full every day for the dawn prayer as they are for the midday Friday prayer, Muslims will be victorious.[a]

Another story goes that in the halcyon days of *al-Andalus* (Muslim Spain c. 711-1492), the "infidels" were looking for the opportune moment to launch their Reconquista. So the king of the infidels sent a man to spy on his enemies. When the man came back, the king asked him:

"What do you have to report?"

"I saw men studying the Quran and talking about *hadith* and *fiqh,*[b]" replied the spy.

"Then it's not the right time to strike them," the king replied and sent him away.

After a while, the king sent out the man again to spy on the Muslims. When he returned, he asked him the same question: "What do you have to report?"

---

[a] I could not find any authentic record of Ben-Gurion actually saying that.

[b] *Fiqh* means Islamic jurisprudence.

"I saw men studying the sciences: medicine, physics, and astronomy."[a]

"Then it's not the right time to strike them," the king replied and sent him away.

Later, the ever so persistent and apparently ageless king, sent out his spy a third time and upon his return repeated the same question. "What do you have to report?"

"I saw men playing music on their musical instruments and singing about their paramours."

"Now is the right time to strike them," the king declared.

If only Muslims had kept their faith and remained true Muslims. Had they done so, they would have remained victorious and unconquerable, or so the narrative goes. By reverting to that state of purity manifested by our ancestors, we would reestablish the most perfect society imaginable, and Muslims would regain their power and status.

That idea is far from original. As late as the 18th century, many Christians essentially believed the same

---

[a] Note how the story, by order of placement, implies that studying medicine, physics, and astronomy are a step down from studying Islamic jurisprudence.

thing – that a populace of true believers would form a perfect society. However, as Jean-Jacques Rousseau pointed out back then, such a society would not be a society of men.[26]

Muslims do not see eye to eye with Rousseau because they hold ahistorical notions about Islamic history. In *Thus Spoke Zarathustra*, Nietzsche famously said that "man is something that is to be surpassed."[27] Muslims believe that man has already been surpassed and that the societies formed by those early Muslim übermensch were utopias. They believe that over the span of 1400 years in which Muslims established several powerful caliphates, Islam was always practiced in some pure, perfect, unadulterated form.

That is categorically false.

Muslim societies in earlier epochs have a checkered past. It is true that they were marked by a level of humanity and social justice that the world had never seen. But there were also dark chapters of religious intolerance, racism, despotism, cronyism, extreme wealth inequality, and even torture. Even if we narrow our focus down to the individual level, we would see that Muslims back then were not always as observant as the average Muslim nowadays is led to believe. For example, drinking wine was a widespread vice. Many caliphs openly ignored Islamic injunctions prohibiting alcohol. Even Ibn Sina[a], the tenth-century polymath extraordinaire and pride of the Muslim community to this very day, indulged in this Bacchic pleasure.

And mind you, Ibn Sina's drinking of wine was not a personal vice of the sort that we are all afflicted with in one shape or form. No, he simply did not believe Islamic law applied to him. He reckoned that Islamic law existed solely "to guide the masses toward Aristotle's Golden Mean of virtuous behavior so that they might purify their souls." It was not meant for those "who had attained true understanding of the nature of reality."[28]

I choose Ibn Sina as an example to show that both faith and its practice were never as pure and unadulterated as Islamic romanticists so often claim. In fact, if Muslim society today were to produce a second Ibn Sina with a similar attitude towards Islam, he would be branded a heretic in many Islamic countries and promptly sent to jail or put to death. Yet the average Joe Muslim nowadays

---

[a] Better known as Avicenna, he was the author of 450 works. His most famous work, *The Canon of Medicine*, is a million-word medical encyclopedia which remained in use as a standard medical text in many medieval universities, as late as 1650 (more than 600 years after his death).

thinks Ibn Sina was some traditionally pious orthodox figure dutifully performing all his Islamic obligations to the letter. If you pointed out the historical reality, he would be either incredulous or indignant.

Even at the time of the Prophet, after the conquest of Mecca, a considerable segment of society was not genuine in their beliefs. Otherwise we would have to concede that people who have been fighting Muhammad and his message for over twenty years underwent an overnight conversion the moment their city was conquered and their idols struck down.

Call me a cynic, but when conversion aligns with material self-interest, it is usually not the legitimate offspring of genuine spiritual conviction but the bastard child of worldly pragmatic concerns.

So the idea of a society comprised of pious Muslim übermensch is a myth. Even at its zenith, Muslim society never lived up fully to the ideals it espoused. A claim otherwise is a willful distortion of history.

Besides, the degree to which the members of a society practice and adhere to their faith is not the sole determinant of how well a society functions. The early years of Islam, which Muslims consider utopic, indeed had many paragons. Many of Muhammad's close companions were genuine in their faith, but they interpreted Islam in different ways. For example, Abu Thar al-Ghafari, one of the early companions of Muhammad, believed that high concentrations of wealth were detrimental to the well-being of the Muslim community. He vehemently argued for the redistribution of wealth among the people. He was a proto-socialist. The fourth caliph, Osman, on the other hand, believed that the annual two-point-five percent *zakat*[a] was enough and did not mind an extreme economic gap between rich and poor[b] or the concentration of wealth in the hands of a select few. Osman was a proto-capitalist. So it is no wonder that Osman and al-Ghafari, both very pious men, hated each other. They both believed in Islam, they

---

[a] *Zakat* is the Muslim annual tax and one of the five pillars of Islam. It's calculated at 2.5% of a Muslim's total savings and wealth above a minimum amount.

[b] A popular folk tale goes that one day the third caliph, Omar, was walking around in disguise in the streets of Mecca when he spotted an old woman cooking for her children. On closer inspection, he noticed that there was nothing in the pot except stones; the woman was only pretending to cook to assuage her hungry children. Deeply moved by this sight, Omar rushed to the nearest granary and brought her flour.

The story is told to demonstrate how Omar cared about his people. The fact that such poverty existed in the first placed, and depended on Omar accidentally passing by to relieve the plight of this old woman and her starving children, is a point often lost on those who retell this story.

Omar was indeed a pious and righteous man, but the society he governed was not a utopia.

both based their opinions on Islamic scripture, they both set out to establish a system of social justice, and yet ironically their views were irreconcilable. They came up with divergent opinions on how best to govern the Muslim community and this divergence ultimately led to open conflict.

In fewer than three decades after the Prophet's death, his closest companions were at each other's throat in the name of the one true God. The nascent Muslim community fell into civil war, the fallout of which we still see today in the Sunni-Shia split.

Islamic societies were never a mythic city of God, because even when their leaders led in his name, these societies were never under the direct sovereignty of God but under the suzerainty of man. They were not ruled by his Divine Will but by the flawed human interpretation thereof. Hence, not only did an Islamic utopia never exist, it never could have existed.

Muslims' belief that the renaissance of Muslim societies is dependent on average Muslims becoming pious übermensch in line with our ancestors and their supposedly glorious utopias leads people down one of two dangerous paths.

The first – and by far the most common – path in Muslim societies is that of despondency and lethargy. People survey the world around them, realize that it is nowhere near the utopic ideal they have in their head, then revert back to their Chekhovian existence. Since renaissance depends on *other* people becoming true Muslims, and since history is moving us towards some preordained victory at the end of time anyway, there is nothing better to do than to wait it out. It is an attitude that subtly shifts responsibility from the individual to the group, thereby freeing its adherent from any sense of guilt he might otherwise feel for failing to act. When God wills it, people will return to their faith, Muslims will be victorious, and virtue, currently meaningless and quixotic, will manifest itself automatically in oneself and in everyone else in that state of perfection. As for when will God will it… well, he will when he does, because there is no rushing God's will. But rest assured, Muslims proclaim, he will will it soon, because we are definitely in the End Times, no question about it.

In the meantime, all that a good little Muslim needs to do is agitate about the plight of Muslims (though only those suffering on the hands of non-Muslims, preferably

Jews), hold the right opinions, and express both as loudly and vehemently as possible.

It is basically *Deus Vult* meets Muslim fatalism with millenarianism and moral exhibitionism thrown in for good measure.

The second path takes a more active but no less pathological approach. We see this trend in ISIS and in the adherents of Salafisim and Wahabisim. Drawing on the notion that early Muslim medieval societies were utopic, they reject the modern world – as if it can be rejected – and embrace an ancient world that exists only in their collective imagination. They grow their beards, wear turbans, and dress in robes. They employ archaic lexicon and syntax in their speech and literature. They give each other Islamic titles like *emir*[a] and w*alli*[b]. And they drop their last names in favor of toponymic surnames as was customary in earlier centuries.[c]

This all sounds benign, like some sort of historical reenactment or period drama, until you realize that having

---

[a] *Emir* means prince in Arabic.

[b] *Walli* is the Arabic title given for the governor of a province.

[c] Not all jihadis are so lucky to get a toponymic surname. One particular jihadi, who also happens to be a dwarf, got stuck with an unflattering nom de guerre: Abu Ahmad al-Chihuahua. He's also called Syrian Lannister.

idealized the past, every foible and injustice that occurred in the past becomes acceptable to those people.

Muslims make a spirited case that the Wahabis and ISIS are not Islamic because they do not represent the values of Islam. They say these groups twist the words of God and his Prophet and that their creed is nothing short of an abomination. True, but the ahistorical idealized outlook of our history that pervades the Muslim world, does in fact contribute to the ISIS/Wahabi phenomenon.

Members of ISIS and followers of the Wahabi interpretation of Islam cannot admit that sexual slavery[a] was inhumane, because to do so would be to break their syllogistic chain of logic.

The Rashidun Caliphate[b] was perfect.

Sexual slavery existed during the Rashidun Caliphate.

Therefore sexual slavery is acceptable, if not good.

---

[a] The concept I am referring to is a*l-Sabi*, which is the Arabic term for the enslavement of women of the losing faction in times of war.

[b] The Rashidun Caliphate was the first caliphate established after the death of the Prophet Muhammad in 632 AD. It was ruled by the first four caliphs, who are collectively known as the *"Rashidun"* or "Rightly Guided" caliphs. Though this period was plagued by civil strife, it is considered by Muslims as a "Golden Age" where adherence to Islamic law and values was at its zenith.

To accept that sexual slavery was inhumane would be to admit that the Rashidun Caliphate was not perfect. That is a notion many pious Muslims would consider blasphemous, and hence they would go to great – and often ridiculous – lengths to challenge any idea that would prove otherwise.

On the website islamweb.net, which answers inquiries about Islam in the form of online fatwas, one person asked why Islam did not forbid sexual slavery.

First the "expert" rebuked the inquirer, falsely claiming that this question did not have any practical value[a] as if even posing the question is in itself wrong, incorrect, or immoral. Then he went on to write this pearl of wisdom about sexual slavery, which I have translated from Arabic:

> Sexual intercourse with a sexual slave does
> not involve rape, nor aggression towards the
> woman, nor a violation of her rights. On the
> contrary it is meant to honor her and
> improve her status because when a sexual
> slave falls under the dominion of a man, she
> often becomes part of his family. And she is

---

[a] Unfortunately, this anti-intellectual bias is quite common in the Muslim world. More on that in Chapter 7.

a woman who has her psychological and sexual needs. So if the man is forbidden from having intercourse with her, then it is temptation for him because she's a foreign woman living with him at his home … day and night. And it is temptation for her considering she has her own needs. Therefore, God allows her master to have intercourse with her so that they don't fall into sin, and so that the sexual slave doesn't resort to indecency and fornication … this constitutes a kind and generous treatment of the sexual slave.[29]

Cicero once quipped that there is nothing so absurd that a philosopher has not already said it. If he were alive today, he could make the same comment about our Muslim scholars. That tragicomic response perfectly illustrates the self-delusion in the Muslim world. Enslaving a woman and raping her, according to our Islamic virtuoso, honors her because in doing so a man is satisfying her "needs." For him, she is a sexual object who, present circumstances be damned, has no concerns except getting laid. The Muslim man who came in with an army, slaughtered her father, husband, and son, pillaged her town, forced her out of her home, and enslaved her is a Don Juan whom she cannot possibly resist. Even if sexual desire had not been burned out of her by the trauma she had suffered, she still would not want her needs satisfied by a man who had a hand in butchering her family.

The Muslim scholar's absurd response stems from his idealization of the past. He believes the past was perfect, and so he pulls off feats of mental gymnastics worthy of a pilpul lawyer in order to justify every practice within Islamic history. The question posed on the website did not require a reckless somersault of rationalization to answer it. It just needed honest analysis unchecked by undue reverence. Sexual slavery was a way to prevent gang-rape and sadism – common occurrences in war, even in modern times. The sexual slavery in the form it was practiced in Muslim societies may have been a lesser evil meant to prevent a greater one, but it was evil nonetheless and it is not something we should glorify or, God forbid, re-institutionalize.

Same goes for the notions of raiding, spoils of war, and ransoms. These were part and parcel of the medieval world, but no more, and good riddance.

At least when it comes to these particular issues, modern societies are more in line with Islam's humanistic values than Muslim societies were at the time of the caliphates. All their other crimes notwithstanding, the United States did not go about enslaving women when they went into Iraq and Afghanistan. And neither does Israel when it raids Gaza. So as far as this particular issue is concerned, America and Israel, the great evil states in the eyes of many Muslims, have a one-up on the caliphates that Muslims glorify as the quintessence of justice.

One is not supposed to idealize the past and slavishly devote themselves to it. One is supposed to study it, learn from it, then build on it.

Unfortunately, that is a narrative that Muslims have yet to internalize.

Chapter 3

Jihad: Trotting Towards a Better World on a Red Horse

Islam was spread by the sword. Well, that is what we keep hearing anyway.

When people think about how Islam spread, what comes to mind? Turban-wearing, bearded warrior savages galloping on horseback. With brandished scimitars and battle cries of *Allahu Akbar*, they swarm into the peaceful lands of the nonbelievers. They rape. They kill. They pillage. They subjugate everyone with fire and steel.

According to Dr. Reza Aslan, religious studies scholar and professor at University of California, this picture is in fact a cliché, which "has its origins in the papal propaganda of the crusades."[30]

But surely Islam is a religion of war; nineteenth-century German sociologist Max Weber tells us that Islam is not a religion of salvation. It is a "warrior religion."[31] Isn't it?

In fact, it is not. "Jihadism" is a politicized, contemporary reading of the concept of jihad. The term jihad which we hear so often does not mean "holy war." It simply means "a struggle" or "a great effort." Now, as Maaajid Nawaz pointed in his interview with Sam Harris, it would be "naïve" to hold that, traditionally, Muslims interpreted jihad as purely "an inner struggle."[32] Islam is not a pacifist religion. It is incumbent on all Muslims to struggle against injustice and tyranny, and so jihad does take a military form in certain contexts. In its most common and applicable form, however, Jihad is a purely spiritual struggle. The term "holy war" does not exist in early Islamic lexicon but was in fact coined by Christian crusaders who wanted to give their war over land and trade a veneer of theological legitimacy. In Islam, war itself can never be holy; it can only be just or unjust.[33]

Verses commanding Muhammad and his followers to "Kill the polytheists wherever you find them" (Quran 9:5) and to "Fight those who do not believe in God or in the

Last Day" (Quran 9:29) were not universal commandments. As Dr. Aslan notes:

> It must be understood that these verses were directed specifically at the Quraysh and their clandestine partisans in Yathrib – specifically named in the Quran as "the polytheists" and "the hypocrites" respectively – with whom the Ummah [the Muslim community] was locked in a terrible war.[34]

Dr. Jonathan Brown, professor of Islamic studies at Georgetown University, makes the same point:

> The Quran's many commands to fight the Arab polytheists until they embraced Islam were the products of a context in which these unbelievers posed an existential threat to Muhammad's new religion.[35]

As does Dr. John Esposito:

> [It] is a distortion to apply this passage to all non-Muslims or unbelievers; the verse is specifically referring to Meccan "idolaters" who are accused of breaking a treaty and continuously warring against the Muslims.[36]

Furthermore, if one compares the violent verses in the Quran to those in the Bible, it is no contest as to which is bloodier. The most violent Quranic verses, mentioned earlier, are still open to a charitable interpretation. One could argue that these verses apply only to adult males who are engaged in hostilities against the Muslim community. Biblical verses of the same ilk, however, leave no wiggle room for a charitable interpretation, as demonstrated by the following verses:

> [Do] not leave alive anything that breathes. Completely destroy them—the Hittites, Amorites, Canaanites, Perizzites, Hivites, and Jebusites—as the Lord your God has commanded you. (Deuteronomy 20:16–17)

> Now go, attack the Amalekites and totally destroy all that belongs to them. Do not spare them; put to death men and women, children and infants, cattle and sheep, camels and donkeys. (1 Samuel 15:3)

> Happy is he who repays you for what you have done to us – he who seizes your infants

and dashes them against the rocks. (Psalm 137:9)

Where is the ambiguity in seizing infants and dashing their brains against rocks?[a][37] How can these verses be construed in any way other than a binding religious duty to commit genocide?

Even if we compare both texts as a whole, the Quran is actually less violent than its Judeo-Christian counterparts. In a study conducted by software engineer Tom Anderson, text analytics software was used to process the Old Testament, the New Testament, and the Quran. What he found is that both the Old and the New Testament are more violent than the Quran, with the Old Testament being "more than twice as violent."[38]

Alright, so even if Islam is not a religion of war, Muhammad was a warlord, was he not?

Not really.

Sam Harris, Ayan Hirsi Ali, the late Christopher Hitchens, and even the eminent Jordan Peterson have

---

[a] According to Bertrand Russell, the Spaniards in Peru and Mexico, perhaps inspired by the aforementioned verses, would dash the brains of native infants against the rocks. But interestingly enough, right before committing that act of barbarity, they would baptize the babies in order to secure their passage into the Kingdom of Heaven.

repeated the claim that Muhammad was a warlord. However, if we look at Muhammad's life, we see that he was, for most of his life, a simple merchant. Muhammad was born in 570 AD. The Battle of Badr, the first "battle"[a] in Islamic history, took place at 623 AD. That means that Muhammad was fifty-three when he first engaged in warfare. And knowing that he died at 632 AD at the age of sixty-two, means Muhammad's entire military career spanned less than nine years.

Even in those nine years, most of the wars he fought were defensive. It was a struggle for survival against the pagan tribes who had placed an embargo on his supporters and would have butchered every last one of them if they had the chance. That is why Muslims did not even control the entire Arabian Peninsula at the time of Muhammad's death.

In total, Muhammad, as Margaret Nydell points out, "fought fewer than 10 battles in his lifetime, resulting in barely 1,000 casualties on both sides."[39] Compare that with the exploits of Alexander, Hannibal, Julius Caesar, Genghis Khan, Napoleon, or even with biblical warrior-prophets

---

[a] I use the term battle in a loose sense. It was really just a tribal skirmish. Muhammad's entire army consisted of 313 infantry and 2 cavalry. Yes, *two* cavalry.

like David, Saul, or Solomon. Juxtaposed against those figures' highlights, Muhammad's warlord cred leaves much to be desired.

Taking these facts into consideration, it is no wonder that the granddaddy of all pacifists, Mahatma Gandhi, had this to say about Muhammad:

> I wanted to know the best of the life of one who holds today an undisputed sway over the hearts of millions of mankind… I became more than ever convinced that it was not the sword that won a place for Islam in those days in the scheme of life. It was the rigid simplicity, the utter self-effacement of the Prophet, the scrupulous regard for pledges, his intense devotion to his friends and followers, his intrepidity, his fearlessness, his absolute trust in God and in his own mission. These and not the sword carried everything before them and surmounted every obstacle. When I closed the second volume (of the Prophet's biography), I was sorry there was not more for me to read of that great life.[40]

So Muhammad was not the bloodthirsty warlord he is often made out to be, and Muslims did not engage in wanton rape and pillage; but Islam still spread by the sword, right?

Yes and no.

But before we get into this, it is important to put things into perspective. Islam was born in an era where conflict between empires was the norm in international relations, not the exception as it is today. By the time the new religion started spreading beyond the Arabian Peninsula, the two world powers at the time – the Byzantines and the Sasanians, both theocratic kingdoms – had already been engaged in a war of attrition with each other for more than a quarter century. Muslims did not bring conflict to a peaceful land; they simply "joined in the existing fracas" and somehow managed to come out on top.[41]

Furthermore, despite their sweeping military victories against the dominant powers at the time, Muslims never compelled people in conquered lands to convert, which was in line with a Quranic principle stating that "there is no compulsion in religion." (2:256) Non-Muslims had to pay an annual tax called *jizyah* but were otherwise free to practice their beliefs.[a] There was no religious persecution on the scale seen in Europe from the time of the reign of Emperor Constantine in the 4th century until the Peace of Westphalia in the middle of the 17th century. During that period, Christians put whole towns to the torch on account of what their residents believed and slaughtered countless people "without regard to sex or old age or infancy."[42] There is nothing analogous to that in Islamic history. Neither were there forced mass conversions like what Christians did to the Saxons, Jews, Moors, Cathars, Kievan Rus, Lithuanians, Incans, Aztecs, and Goans. The Ottoman Empire, for example, had "twenty people with different religions."[43] Jacobites, Nestorians, Monothelites, Copts, Christians of St. John, Maronites, Druze, Shiites, Alevis, Jews, and Zoroastrians coexisted in relative peace for centuries. Yes, there were occasional persecutions but as the eminent historian of Islam Bernard Lewis noted,

---

[a] In modern anti-Islamic rhetoric, we often hear about the evil of the *jizyah* system. Though it was certainly abused at times by rulers looking to swell the imperial treasury, in theory, it wasn't a terrible burden on those who chose to retain their faith. It only applied to free adult males. Women, children, the elderly, the handicapped, the ill, the insane, monks, hermits, slaves, and adult males who chose to do military service were all exempt. Even anyone who just couldn't pay was exempt too. To put things into perspective, compare that system with the tax code in England, where Catholics had to pay double taxes and were barred from office until 1829. Even when held up to modern day standards, certain aspects of it fare quite well. Would the IRS – or any modern tax system – be so progressive as to exempt people from tax just for not being able to afford it?

such instances "were rare, and usually of brief duration, related to local and specific circumstances."[44] So Islam did not spread by the sword, in the convert-or-die sense that is often assumed.

However, the domain of political Islam, i.e. lands where Islam was the state religion, was established to a large extent by military conquest.[a]

That is not a badge of shame on Islam or Muslims. Islam is a religion, and back then you could not establish a religion without also establishing a domain in which it could be freely practiced and propagated. It is not like Muhammad could upload some YouTube videos and see people flock to his message. As Jean-Jacques Rousseau points out, "Religion was attached… to the state that prescribed it, [hence] the only missionaries there could be were conquerors."[45] There was no peaceful means to proselytize effectively, period.

At that time, military expansion was synonymous with proselytizing and survival. Muslims back then realized that, which is why they divided the world into two

----

[a] I am aware that this doesn't apply everywhere across the globe. Southeast Asia for example, where the majority of Muslims live nowadays, underwent no military conquest but rather converted on their own due to the influence of Muslim merchants. Cases like these are the exception though, not the rule.

categories: *dar al islam* (House of Islam) and *dar al harb* (House of War). That worldview was not rooted in religious doctrine but in *realpolitik*. Had Muslims not sought out to establish a political domain, they would not have been able to get their message across to many people. Islam would have eventually been wiped out by another ideology unburdened with hippy sensibilities.

People often bring up Christianity as a counter to the previous point. They claim Jesus was a pacifist on account of him saying, "But I say unto you, That ye resist not evil: but whosoever shall smite thee on thy right cheek, turn to him the other also." (Matthew 5:39) Seems like a dyed-in-the-wool flower child. That is, until a few chapters down the line when you get to (Matthew 10:34): "Think not that I come to send peace on earth: I came not to send peace, but a sword." Suddenly Jesus does not appear to be such a pacifist after all. This shows that the previous verse was perhaps not a universal commandment as it is often understood. Had Jesus been born in a world as multipolar as the one Muhammad was born into and lived as long as him, things might have turned out differently. Perhaps Jesus would have eventually picked up a spear and locked it with the Roman gladius.

Anyway, scriptural distinctions and alternative historical musings aside, the fact remains that Christianity only managed to spread after Emperor Constantine converted and it gained the full might of the Byzantine Empire behind it. This culminated during the reign of Emperor Theodosius II, who issued the following edict in his *Codex Theodosianus*:

> It is Our will that all the people who are ruled by the administration of Our Clemency shall practice that religion which the divine Peter the Apostle transmitted to the Romans... We command that those persons who follow this rule shall embrace the name of Catholic Christians. The rest, however, whom we adjudge demented and insane, shall sustain the infamy of heretical dogmas, their meeting places shall not receive the name of churches, and they shall be smitten first by divine vengeance and secondly by the retribution of Our own initiative.[46]

For the first three hundred years of its existence, Christianity was not backed by a military force. This was not to the benefit of the fledgling faith. Because of its minority status, Christianity could not keep the established ancient mystery religions from leaving their taint on its creed – a taint that runs far deeper than Easter bunnies and Christmas trees. Mary's portrayal as the mother of God draws heavily from the pagan goddess Ishtar. While Jesus's portrayal as her son who is killed and is reborn is based on the pagan god Adonis. If Christianity had been able to assert itself as the state religion sooner, it is quite likely that Christianity would be fundamentally different at a doctrinal level than it is today.

Furthermore, due to a lack of state backing in its formative years, Christianity had no centralized leadership. Christians operated as disparate cells. That is why they ended up with interpretations that differ from each other on key tenets of faith. Had Christians been able to develop a state-backed orthodoxy, there would be far fewer denominations in the Christian world. Incidentally, Europe would also have been spared centuries of religious wars and bloodshed.

But I digress.

We have established thus far that militant jihad is not rooted in scripture or the example set by Muhammad. Yet there is no denying that there does exist in the Muslim world a *dangerous narrative* that sees militant jihad as the way forward. One can see this clearly in the works of 20th century Islamists like Sayyid Qutb[a] (the ideologue who inspired Usama Bin Laden) and Hassan al-Banna, founder of the Muslim Brotherhood. And that narrative is not limited to theorists. At least a portion of the population upholds this view.

So where does this *dangerous narrative* come from?

Both anti-Muslim polemicists and Islamists cherry pick verses from the Quran and events from the life of Muhammad to draw a causal relationship between those and militant jihadism, but as I have demonstrated earlier in this chapter, that explanation does not hold.

I propose that modern-day militant jihadism, as an idea, rests on two pillars. The first one is a hagiographic and selective reading of early Islamic history that emphasizes and glorifies the military conquests of that period above every other achievement or consideration. Muslim youth are weaned on stories of the battles of early

---

[a] Though he provided jihadist groups with ideological narratives and frameworks, to be fair, Sayyid Qutb never advocated the killing of innocents and would have been appalled by what some of his radical followers have carried out in his name. To lay the blame fully at his doorstep would be like laying the blame at Rousseau for the Reign of Terror because Robespierre and the Jacobins appropriated his philosophy and used some of his words as battle cries during their bloody revolution.

Islamic history. They know all the details about the battles of Badr and Uhud, and the conquest of Mecca. They know about Ali, Muhammad's cousin, and his great feats of strength on the battlefield. They know about the military genius Khalid ibn al-Walid and his exploits against the numerically superior forces of the Sasanians and the Byzantines. They know about Tariq ibn Ziyad, who crossed the Straits of Gibraltar (which are named after him) and, with a small force, managed to conqueror Spain, thereby ushering in 700 years of Muslim rule in the Iberian Peninsula.

For most Muslims, the formative years of Islamic history are like a Michael Bay Hollywood summer blockbuster – an adrenaline-denominated sequence of military conquests and feats of courage on the battlefield. Few know that that was not really the case. The formative years of Islam were really about pushing for social and economic changes to challenge the mores of a society characterized by improper distribution of wealth and rampant injustice. Also, not everyone back then was a warrior for Islam. There were in fact all types of people who performed all sorts of functions.

But alas, all that lives on in the minds of Muslims today is the archetype of the warrior and his feats on the field of battle. All else has been dangerously marginalized. So while courage, bravery, and sacrifice are celebrated, non-martial values like work ethic, self-restraint, responsibility, and learning – values that are crucial to the functioning and prosperity of civil society – do not command the same prestige in the Muslim psyche.

Furthermore, when Muslims reflect on the military campaigns throughout Islamic history, they do so in a manner that is completely uncritical. Muslims' unquestioning glorification of Islamic conquests have rendered them blind to the terrible human tragedy that underlies all wars. I am not a tree-hugging pacifist; I believe that war is sometimes necessary. But to sanitize war, to make it look pristine whereas it is in fact ugly and brutal is foolhardy; and this is exactly what Muslims have been doing in the way they portray their history.

The second pillar upon which the *dangerous narrative* extolling modern-day militant jihadism rests is the fundamental misunderstanding of the dynamics of modern war. Reading Islamist thinkers like the aforementioned Qutb and al-Banna, one is struck by the notion that they really do not understand modern war. For them and other Islamist ideologues, war has not changed since feudal times. For starters, they view war not as the domain of professional soldiers but of zealous volunteers, as if manpower were the sole deciding factor in modern war. Even in World War I, that mentality was obsolete. The generals of that conflict sent millions of raw conscripts to their deaths in massed infantry charges, and yet trench lines barely moved for the duration of the war. Today in the age of drones, tanks, and attack helicopters, that stratagem is more irrelevant than it has ever been.

Moreover, they still believe that war, if waged successfully, is a path to economic prosperity and political power. For most of human history, from ancient Rome to the days of Queen Victoria, that notion was true. In the 19th century, the British Empire, along with France, Germany, Portugal, Belgium, Italy, and Spain, owed much of its wealth and power to the spoils that it seized from its colonies. The advent of modern armaments at the beginning of the 20th century, however, completely overturned the equation. War was no longer the forge of nations but rather their death knell, even for the victors. Despite winning both World Wars, the British Empire – once dubbed "the empire on which the sun never sets" – was reduced to an island nation consigned to playing second fiddle to greater powers. Even small wars can sap a nation's vitality and hobble its growth.

In 2014, Russian forces invaded Ukraine and annexed Crimea. From a military perspective, it was a masterstroke. Russia captured a major naval stronghold on the Black Sea, which is of vital strategic importance – and it did so without suffering any losses. From a political perspective, the invasion was no less impressive, as it allowed the Kremlin to reassert itself as a force to be reckoned with. But despite all that, was it worth it? Was it worth the heavy economic sanctions and the political isolation?

The economic data speaks for itself. Russia's sputtering economy had an average growth rate of 1.2% over the last ten years. In comparison, the Eurozone averaged 2.5%, the United States 2.3%[47], and China, which did not let its geopolitical ambitions embroil it in some military adventure, averaged more than 8% growth over the same period.[48]

War simply does not pay off like it used to. That is why England did not send troops to Scotland to lay waste to Edinburgh when the Scots decided to hold an independence referendum. That is why China did not blockade Taiwan with its powerful navy and pummel the small island nation into submission. And that is why Israel did not just dispatch a large contingent of Merkava tanks to level Gaza into an oversized parking lot, thereby answering the Palestinian Question once and for all. Humanity did not become enlightened and transcend petty conflicts. If the dynamics of war and world politics were the same today as they were in the 19th century, Israel would have long since captured Damascus, Beirut, and Cairo. There wouldn't be Syria, Lebanon, or Egypt, much less Gaza or the West Bank. It is not that they lack the means to do so. It is just that war is not worth it anymore. Its costs often dwarf whatever little benefit can be scraped from it. Economics is the great Leviathan that keeps all the states in check.

Another point that Islamists do not seem to grasp about modern war is that while starting a war is easy, winning one is expensive. Victory requires a massive economic bedrock and manufacturing infrastructure. Japan did not lose the Second World War because their soldiers were inferior. If *kamikaze* attacks were any indication, Japanese soldiers were probably braver, or at least more dedicated, than their American counterparts. They lost the war because they were economically outmatched. The production capacity, resources, and material wealth of the continental United States vastly outstripped those of Imperial Japan. Even if the atomic bomb had not been invented, in fact even if Pearl Harbor was a monumental success and the Japanese had been able to take out all the battleships, all the carriers, and all the facilities on the island, the US would have still ultimately won the war. That is because, as Admiral Yamamoto stated prior to the attack on Pearl Harbor, "Should hostilities break out between Japan the United States, it is not enough that we take Guam and the Philippines, nor even Hawaii and San Francisco. We would have to march into Washington and sign the treaty in the White House."[49] Since such a scenario was not possible under any circumstance, absent a Hail Mary pass in the form of some Japanese super weapon, The Empire of the Rising Sun lost the very moment it declared war.

In light of that, calls for jihad by the likes of Qutb, al-Banna, and their ideological disciples ring not only of futility but of folly, as if we are being called upon to heap our own funeral pyre. During the Bambatha rebellion at the beginning of the 20th century, Zulu warriors armed with *assegai* spears and cowhide shields fought the forces of the British Empire. The colonial soldiers, who were armed with rifles, machine guns, and canons, soundly defeated the insurgents. They took out three to four thousand Zulu warriors while losing only 36 of their own men.[50] This is what would transpire should the morbid dreams of Islamists come to fruition – not an Islamic utopia but senseless slaughter of their own people.

Islamists also do not realize that other nations would not tolerate a country whose *modus operandi* is annexing any territory it can seize by force, as though it still exists in a state of nature. For such a state is a state of war. As Thomas Hobbes notes, war does not necessarily entail fighting. War is the mere "disposition to fight during a time when there is no assurance to the contrary."[51] Immanuel Kant is his essay, *Toward Perpetual Peace*, explains the effect of such a state:

> A man… in the state of nature… harms me
> – even if he doesn't do anything to me – by
> the mere fact that he isn't subject to any
> laws and is therefore a constant threat to
> me.[52]

Though this particular paragraph talks about individuals, it is applicable to nation states, and Kant affirms that later in his essay. In the past, all nations existed in a state of nature, but things have changed. The Peace of Westphalia in 1648 led to the development of a national consciousness in Europe that saw itself as part of a wider world. Political entities were no longer regarded as powers to be subsumed but as independent states with precise lines of demarcation. That consciousness has of course developed since its inception. Now, even the United States, the most powerful country in the world with a military budget equal to that of the rest of the world put together, requires a *casus belli* before it can resort to arms. Whether the pretext is real or manufactured is beside the point – the fact that it needs one shows that the rules governing international relations have changed.

However, many Muslims' understanding of international politics is stuck in the past. They still yearn for a return of the age of conquests when caliphs used to go on military campaigns every other year. The leader of the well-funded militant group Lashkar e-Taiba in Pakistan openly stated in an interview that the aim of his group was to "unfurl the green flag of Islam in Washington, Tel Aviv, and New Delhi."[53] Variations of that declaration, similar in both content and form, have been heard from like-minded individuals throughout the Muslim world. For example, in Palestine, Sheikh Abu Hanifa Awda made a similar statement in a speech he gave recently at al-Aqsa Mosque in Jerusalem. In that speech, he talked about a day when Muslims will send brigades to conqueror the world – including one to liberate Palestine, one to take revenge on

Russia, one to liberate the Muslim world, one to lay siege to Rome, one to turn the White House black, one to impose tribute on London, and one to take over the Rockies and the Andes.[54]

A state committed to territorial expansion like the one Lashkar e-Taiba, Sheikh Awda, and many Muslims envision would not only pose a threat to the security and stability of its neighbors but it would also cripple them economically. After all, there is no incentive for major capital investment in a place under constant threat of invasion and ruin. Hence, a state with that approach to international politics would not be allowed to exist – and with good reason.

Finally, Islamist rhetoric is marked by an absence of any reflection on the moral implications of harming civilians. It is not an oversight born of callousness. On the contrary, you will often find these thinkers praising Islam's humanitarian rules of conduct in times of war and noting that God "instructs Muslims to act with the utmost mercy."[55] Islamic rules of engagement, after all, forbid Muslims, *inter alia*, to kill any child, woman, or elderly person, uproot or burn a tree, slaughter livestock, kill anyone taking refuge in a place of worship, destroy a village or town, spoil cultivated fields or gardens, or even to strike someone on the face.[56]

It is just that they do not seem to understand that all these things that Islam strictly prohibits are part and parcel of modern war. Gone are the days of limited scale engagements between combatants arrayed neatly in formation against each other, where death and suffering were constrained to the field of battle.

In modern war, collateral damage is inevitable. The pregnant mother, the infant child, and the elderly matron are just as likely to suffer as the soldier on the field. And the fate they suffer is often a grim one… far worse than a "strike on the face."

Islamists never stop to pause and think that the global jihad they advocate would result in immeasurable human suffering if it ever came to fruition – countless women, children, and elderly burned, dismembered, and mutilated.

It is a graphic picture. But it is the truth. This is war. It is not an armored knight on horseback, a brave man scaling battlements, or even a resolute soldier in a trench. The sheer destructiveness of modern armaments precludes any possibility of a clean offensive war with no civilian casualties.

It is these pillars more than anything else that allow militant jihadism to be seen as a viable option. Any piece of scripture or *hadith* plucked out of context (by disregarding historical circumstances) and out of text (by disregarding how it fits with the rest of the Quran and *hadith*) to make a case for militant jihadism is not the root cause of that ideology but merely a sham justification of it. As for the dangers of such a narrative, there are several.

First, it instills in young Muslims the idea that giving up one's life for a cause is the greatest sacrifice a person can make. That may be true when a cause is facing an existential physical threat, as was the case at the time. In today's age, however, the greatest sacrifice and ultimate expression of faith is not to opt out of life in a puff of fire and smoke as solitary, lonely, misfit, depressed young Muslims expediently choose to believe. The greatest sacrifice is to live life to its fullest – both morally and socially – to strive to do good and move this world a bit closer to heaven while also navigating the complexities, pressures, and tribulations of modern life.

Second, it blinds Muslims to solutions for geopolitical predicaments that do not involve war.

Abraham Maslow once said, "if all you have is a hammer, everything looks like a nail." I would like to propose another sociological theory: if all you have is a sword – or an ideology that revolves around it – everyone looks like an infidel.

Just read Sayyid Qutb and you will see the problem. His ideology is disturbingly single minded. His seminal work, *Milestones*[57], which was meant as a road map to a vanguard of Muslims to bring forth a better future, does not concern itself at all with education or politics. Neither does he give much thought to economics. In fact, he outright admits that the West is so far ahead materially that it is futile to try to catch up. Instead, for all the Muslim world's problems he proposes a singular solution: jihad. Jihad against the state and jihad against the whole world. It is a dangerous *idée fixe* and the reason no one in the Muslim world can, for example, come up with a solution to the Arab-Israeli conflict that does not involve conquest and Armageddon.

Third, the current mindset fosters an attitude of appropriation and usurpation. It is not actually an Islamic mindset. It is a mindset that is at its core Bedouin and tribal.[a] It is the mindset of the resource-strapped desperado, whose only chance at survival is winning the zero-sum game against all the other Bedouin desperadoes. If he needs a goat, a camel, or a horse, he needs to steal it. Ditto if he needs a wife.

Except the modern world is not a Hobbesian state of nature where everything is up for grabs if only one has the power to grab it. Success, nowadays, requires a different mindset. It requires a mindset that fosters productivity, achievement, and conscientiousness. Only then can we transition from a society where the law of the wild rules supreme to one built on principles of justice and egalitarianism.

Fourth, it creates an us-versus-them mentality, a Manichean worldview that justifies endless perpetual conflict. Good versus evil. Again we turn to Qutb. For him, there are no shades of gray. The world is divided into two polarities. The World of Islam and the World of *Jahiliya* (ignorance and barbarism). Any society that does not dedicate itself to the "submission" to God in its "beliefs, ideas, and observances of worship, and in its legal

---

[a] That's why the Arabic word for occupation, *mihna*, gets its root from the Arabic word for humiliation.

regulations"[58] is a barbaric pagan society that must be "annihilated." [59] And thus Muslims must engage in perpetual conflict until all the world is under the banner of Islam and the sovereignty of God.

Most Muslims would not put it in such stark terms as Qutb did. But they have internalized that narrative, albeit in milder form. For many Muslims, the world is us-versus-them. That is why it is hard for the Muslim psyche to truly picture a viable future of peace and co-existence. Even if they truly wish for it, deep down they do not think it is possible. We are setting ourselves up to be at war with all people for all eternity.

In the book of Genesis, we find the following verse about Ishmael, from whom Arabs descended:

> He will be a wild donkey of a man; his hand will be against everyone and everyone's hand will be against him; and he will live in hostility against all his brothers. (Genesis 16:12)

This is actually a mistranslation. As noted in the book, *Jesus: Man, Messenger, Messiah,* the Hebrew word used for "wild donkey" (*pereh* or *pere*) is similar to another Hebrew word, *para,* which means fruitful. And the word "against" is a single consonant in Hebrew which could also mean: "in, at, to, on, among, with, towards, according to, by, because of."[60]

So what the Bible actually says is: "He will be a fruitful man; his hand shall be with everyone, and every man's hand shall be with him…"[a] This is how the sons of Ishmael are supposed to live. They should be living hand-in-hand with the rest of humanity.

This is not a pipe dream. As noted by Omar Saif Ghobash, the UAE ambassador to Russia, if Muslims demonstrate "grace and patience in the face of imagined, or actual, slights" then they are "likely to defuse the animosity that others may have" towards them.[61] It is possible to live in harmony with non-Muslim states.

So how does one disabuse Muslims of their fascination with militant jihad? Well, I am tempted to offer the solution proposed by George Orwell in his war memoir, *Homage to Catalonia*, written during the Spanish Civil

---

[a] This translation is corroborated by the Bible since in Genesis 17:20 it is the Hebrew word *para* that is used to describe Ishmael: "As for Ishmael, I have heard of thee: behold I have blessed him, and will make him fruitful, and will multiply him exceedingly; twelve princes shall he beget, and I will make him a great nation."

In the Samaritan Torah, we also find Ishmael described in a positive light: "He will be fertile of man. His hand will be with everyone. And everyone's hand will be with him. And he will live among all his brothers."

War.[a][62] On a more serious note, however, I believe the first step would be to topple the pillars upon which this narrative stands. Muslims must learn to appreciate the non-martial accomplishments of their history. They should recall that in the days of Muhammad, those who adopted Islam in times of peace were far more numerous than those who adopted it in times of war. That is because Islam flourishes in peace, not war.

They also need to understand that modern war is not analogous with pre-modern military jihad. The sheer destructiveness and butchery of modern war violate Islam's strict rules of engagement. Hence, it is not something to covet.

Regardless what Islamist thinkers purport, Renaissance does *not* hinge on armed struggle. That is a false mirage and a *dangerous narrative* – one that will see a region already mired with backwardness sink into deeper destitution.

---

[a]In this book, he suggests that pacifists should illustrate their pamphlets with enlarged pictures of human lice which resemble tiny lobsters and favor a man's trousers for living and breeding. "Glory of war, indeed!" he writes. "In war all soldiers are lousy... The men who fought at Verdun, Waterloo, at Flodden, at Senlac, at Thermopylae - every one of them had lice crawling over his testicles."

Chapter 4

Palestine: A Land of Olive Trees and No Olive Branch

In 1948, Jewish Zionists established the State of Israel in Palestine. After millennia of persecution, blood libels, expulsions, forced conversions, massacres, and pogroms which culminated in one of the worst atrocities humanity has ever witnessed, the Jewish diaspora finally had their Zion, their sanctuary. Never again would they have to say "Never Again."

For Jews, it was a dream come to true.

To the local Palestinians, however, it was a bloody nightmare, for establishing the State of Israel necessitated getting rid of the local Palestinians. To force the local populace to flee, Jewish paramilitary militias embarked on a campaign of terror. In Deir Yassin, up to two hundred civilians mostly women, children, and old men were killed – many shot execution style to the back of the head.[63] In Lydda, hundreds were killed when armored cars raided the city "spraying machine-gun fire at anything that moved"[64] after which more than a hundred men were rounded up in a mosque and massacred. [65] In al-Dawayima, hundreds, including women and children, were killed in barbarous ways. Children were killed by smashing their skulls with sticks. Elderly women were locked up inside their homes, which were then set up with explosives and blown up. In one case, a woman was forced to serve the troops and clean after them. When it was time for them to move out, they shot her point blank along with her day-old infant and left their carcasses behind to rot.[66]

In the end, more than 530 Palestinian villages were destroyed,[67] and as historian Ilan Pappé notes, "Thousands of Palestinians were killed ruthlessly and savagely by Israeli troops of all backgrounds, ranks, and ages."[68]

Getting wind of these massacres, more than 700,000 Palestinians fled their homes, thinking they would return when things settled down.

Little did they know, that day would never come.

After the hostilities ceased. The newly formed state of Israel permanently barred the fleeing Palestinians from returning and brought in Jewish settlers to take over their homes.

To this day, Palestinian refugees and their descendants, numbering over seven million, are denied the right of return. Israel argues that it cannot be both Jewish and democratic if it lets Palestinians back in.

The events which happened then and the continued occupation of this tract of land are not just salient issues for the Palestinians. These issues occupy center stage in the Muslim psyche and act as a lightning rod to all their grievances. Why? Because this tract of land is not just any tract of land. Barring the century for which it was occupied during the Crusades, this land had always been in Muslim hands since the birth of Islam. It lies at the center of what Muslims see as their homeland – and it contains Jerusalem, the third holiest city in Islam, second only to Mecca and Medina. That is why for Muslims, not just for Palestinians, the events of 1948 are referred to as *al-Nakba,* which means "catastrophe" or "cataclysm." To Muslims, the occupation of the Holy Land and the plight of the Palestinians are the most glaring manifestations of everything wrong in the world and the first thing that must be tackled to set things straight.

Israel's conduct over the past 70 years continues to make matters worse. As noted by professor Francis Boyle, of the 149 substantive articles of the Fourth Geneva Convention that protect the rights of Palestinians, Israel is currently violating almost all of them, and it has been doing so since 1967. [69] This has understandably hardened Muslims' attitude towards Israel.

"Carthago delenda est." During the third Punic War, Roman Senator Cato the Elder repeated that phrase over and over again on the senate floor. "Carthage must be destroyed."

In the Muslim psyche, the same applies for Israel. For Muslims, there can be no diplomatic settlement or peaceful coexistence. To start with, Israel does not even want peace. And besides, Israel was born in an act of ethnic cleansing, and it stands on stolen land, hence its very existence is an abomination. Justice can only be fulfilled when the State of Israel ceases to exist. This is the *dangerous narrative* we are going to explore in this chapter.

Now to make things clear, when I say in the Muslim psyche, Israel must cease to exist, I do not mean that Muslims are itching for a second Holocaust. It is a common refrain in pro-Israeli media that Muslims want to drive Jews into the sea.[70][a] That is not the common Muslim narrative. Even in Iran, which is purportedly driven by genocidal antisemitism, that is not true. Otherwise there wouldn't be 30,000 Jews living there (who, by the way, have turned down all incentives to immigrate offered to them by Israel).[71]

The common narrative is that the State of Israel occupies Palestinian – or Muslim – land and hence should cease to exist in this particular location as a prerequisite for peace and justice. There are no calls for genocide or ethnic cleansing, as many would have you believe.

One could argue that an end to Israel would necessarily entail an act of ethnic cleansing, and thus calling for the former is tantamount to calling for the latter.

---

[a] In 1973, British MP Christopher Mayhew offered £5,000 to anyone who could produce evidence of any genocidal statement by an Arab Leader (The Guardian, 9 September 1974). No one was able to cash in on the reward.

More recently, even the leader of Hamas, Ismail Hanieh, made a statement clarifying their position: "Hamas is not hostile to Jews because they are Jews. We are hostile to them because they occupied our land and expelled our people. We did not say we want to throw the Jews in the sea … We just said that there is a land called occupied Palestine. It was burglarized and it needs to be returned to the Palestinian people."

Logically, that would be true. Jews in Israel cannot be peacefully spirited away to some uninhabited island where they can set up their state. Many Israelis living in Israel are second- and third-generation Israelis. They were born in Israel. Crimes of their fathers notwithstanding, this is not just their home, it is the only home they know. Uprooting them would have to be at least as bloody as the campaign that drove out the Palestinians in 1948.

For most Muslims, however, the issue of Palestine does not exist on a cerebral plain but on an emotional one – a plain that allows Muslims to believe that they could force Israel out of existence while also doing so in a humane manner.

The illogicality inherent in these two beliefs, however, is just a part of the problem. To fully understand the baleful consequences of the *dangerous narrative* stated earlier, we need to step back just a few years before *al-Nakba*. But we are not going to be looking at Palestine; instead, we are going to be looking at Germany.

Nemmersdorf, Germany, 1944.

On the night of October 20th 1944, the residents of Nemmersdorf lay fast asleep in their snug warm beds when they got a rude awakening to the horrors of war. The Red

Army, having punched a hole in the German line, burst into the Reich and swarmed the village and the surrounding countryside. Accounts of what the Soviets did there are harrowing.

They crucified women naked on barn doors and sawed old men who tried to protect their daughters and granddaughters in half. Scores of women and children were squashed flat by tanks. Babies had their heads bashed in. And every female, including girls as young as eight, was raped.[72]

And worst thing is, Nemmersdorf was just a faint foretaste of what lay ahead.

On the Western front, the British and Americans launched massive air raids. Cities all across Germany including Berlin, Nuremberg, Hamburg, Darmstadt, Cologne, Stuttgart, Würzburg, and Munich were bombed gratuitously. Schools, churches, hospitals, and homes were leveled to the ground.

This bombing campaign culminated in the firebombing of Dresden. This city, referred to back then as "Florence on the Elbe," was one of the world's greatest cultural treasures. It had no military or strategic importance.

Yet it was carpet bombed with incendiary explosives.[a] The ensuing firestorm there was so hot that people melted like wax. In Dresden alone, between two hundred to four hundred thousand people met their end in such a grotesque manner.

Over on the Eastern front, terror did not come from the skies. There it marched on land as the endless waves of the Bolshevik armies surged into Germany's hinterland. Prominent Soviet intellectual Ilya Ehrenburg urged his countrymen:

> The Germans are not human beings... Kill them all, men, old men, children and the women after you have amused yourself with them! Kill. Nothing in Germany is guiltless, neither the living nor the yet unborn... Break the racial pride of the German woman. Take her as your legitimate booty. Kill, you brave soldiers of the victorious Soviet Army.[73]

---

[a] The reason Dresden was obliterated in such a brutal manner was that Churchill wanted to demonstrate to Stalin that Britain was still a force to be reckoned with. A quarter million people, mostly women and children, were immolated to make that point.

And so with the blessing of their genocidal ideologues, the Red Army enacted their savage fantasies, and the most depraved of the depraved had a field day. Across the Baltic as well as in Silesia, Prussia, Pomerania, Czechoslovakia, Romania, Hungary, and Yugoslavia, wherever the Soviets occupied German soil or encountered German communities, they went on a rampage of wanton murder and rape.

In his book *Hellstorm*, Thomas Goodrich writes, "Girls, women, and nuns were raped incessantly for hours on end, the soldiers standing in queues, the officers at the head of the queues, in front of their victims… for a female to be ravished one hundred times a week was not uncommon." Russian soldiers even went so far as to violate the corpses.[74]

Meanwhile in Czechoslovakia, people turned torture into a folk festival. German women were tied to advertising poles along with their children and burned alive while spectators cheered and hooted. Others were tied to trucks and dragged across the streets until they were mangled into one big lump of blood, flesh, and dirt.[75] Similar examples of sheer brutality took place across Germany, and purges like the one in Czechoslovakia took place in Hungary, Romania, and Yugoslavia.

Then the war ended. Germany's nightmare, though, was far from over. The Americans "secretly favored a Carthaginian approach to the conquered Reich," so Germany was made to suffer what Time Magazine called "history's most terrifying peace."[76]

First the country was completely plundered. Gold, silver, and precious art were stolen. Factories and plants were likewise dismantled and commandeered.[77]

Then the populace were deliberately starved in a murderous program which was described by William Henry Chamberlain as a "positively sadistic desire to inflict the maximum suffering on all Germans, irrespective of their responsibility for Nazi crimes."[78] So dire were the conditions that "by the summer of 1945, Germany had become the world's greatest slave market where sex was the new medium of exchange."[79] Even the children were selling themselves to stave off starvation.[80] And all of Germany "was a little better than a vast concentration camp."[81]

As for the millions of Germans living outside the newly redrawn borders, they were uprooted from land they had inhabited for 700 years, and their farms and properties were confiscated. Homeless and penniless, they were sent on a long death march back to Germany. Of the eleven million Germans hurled from their homes in Prussia, Pomerania, and Silesia, an estimated two million expellees, mostly women and children, perished. Another million died during similar expulsions from Czechoslovakia, Hungary, Romania, Bulgaria, and Yugoslavia. That is all on top of four million POWs who were sent to Russia to work and die in the Gulags.[82]

Overall, it is estimated that more Germans died during the first two years of "peace" than during the previous six years of war.[83]

Such were the macabre conditions in *post*-war Germany.

The German people had every reason to be bitter and hateful towards their enemies. After all, most of the victims were innocent and had nothing to do with the Holocaust, or the unconscionable crimes perpetrated by the Nazis. And yet, as German POW Hans Woltersdorf observed at the time:

> One element almost totally lacking in the German heart, during the post-war years was surprisingly, the spirit of hatred and revenge. In their heedless, headlong struggle to

survive, there simply was no time or energy left in Germans to dwell on what was or what might have been.[84]

Instead, they threw themselves at work. They cleared the rubble, they rebuilt, and despite all the suffering and sheer inhumanity that they had been subjected to, they prevailed. As Woltersdorf put it, "They achieved a miracle, an economic miracle…"

Now, less than seventy-five years later, Germany is not just rebuilt, it stands as one of the most advanced nations on Earth. Its citizens enjoy a standard of living better than that of its past conquerors. And this time around, refugees are not fleeing Germany, they are risking life and limb to get *into* Germany.

All in the span of seventy-five years.

Now imagine if Germany had adopted the modern Muslim narrative of resistance and perpetual warfare. Imagine that instead of unconditional surrender, they had retreated to the Alps and continued the conflict from there, engaging the Allied forces in brutal guerrilla warfare[85][a].

---

[a] The Alpine Redoubt was a real plan by Heinrich Himmler. It involved retreating to a massive underground fortress in the Alps and continuing the fight on strategically advantageous ground. The plan was never fully endorsed by Hitler.

Imagine that rather than rebuilding their homes, schools, hospitals, and factories, they had diverted their energy into creating makeshift V2 rockets in their cellars to lob at London, Paris, and Moscow. Imagine if they had focused all their attention on reclaiming ancestral provinces that had been stripped away from them. Imagine if they had spent their days attacking checkpoints and throwing rocks and seeking to make the Allies answer for the unspeakable crimes they had perpetrated against them.

Imagine if they had internalized the narrative that they were oppressed, that they were victims. Imagine if they had dubbed the fall of the Reich *"die Katastrophe"* or the expulsion of many Germans from their ancestral lands *"die Vertreibung,"* and then spent the next eight decades ruminating on it.

Where would Germany be today? Why, of course… Germany would be Palestine.

The occupation would have been harsher, as the Allies would have utilized more brutal means to root out resistance movements. No proper infrastructure would have been rebuilt, resources would have been diverted to armed resistance, and anything built would have been destroyed anyway in counter-insurgency operations. The standard of living would have remained at an abyssal low. The new generation would have been raised semi-illiterate due to the lack of proper educational facilities. Petty, opportunistic Führers would have sprung up, each claiming to carry on the fight, while oppressing their own people. Emboldened by their weakness, the Soviet Union and France would have annexed vast tracts of land under the guise of creating a safe border zone. Meanwhile, Germans would have continued voicing their vehement objection to these land grabs and the depopulation measures they entailed.

So yes, it would have been Palestine.

The same argument could be made for Japan. They had two atomic bombs dropped on them. Nearly 200,000 civilians were incinerated in Hiroshima and Nagasaki, and 130,000 civilians were burned to death during the firebombing of Tokyo.[86]

And yet, just like the Germans, they did not focus on revenge. They focused on rebuilding. They even established friendly relations with their conquerors. And now, both stand testimony to the power of human will to rise from the ashes.

I know what Palestinians went through was horrible. And I know they face systemic injustices to this day. There is no denying that. It would be disingenuous, however, to claim that what Palestinians went through and continue to go through on a national level is in some way unique or even comparable to what the Germans and the Japanese endured.

The case of Palestine has strong parallels to the cases of Germany and Japan. They all suffered grave injustices, they were all occupied for a long period of time, and they all had nearly the same time to recover.

And yet, Germany and Japan are now two of the most advanced nations on Earth. They are beacons of egalitarianism, humanitarianism, and democracy that command praise and admiration from the rest of the world. While Palestine and the rest of the Arab world are still petty banana republics and absolute monarchies that, as Egyptian Nobel Peace Prize winner Mohammad ElBaradei put it, "add nothing to humanity or science."[87]

But let's keep throwing rocks shall we, because… oppression.

Article 13 in the original Hamas Charter states:

Initiatives, and so called peaceful solutions and international conferences, are in contradiction to the principles of the Islamic

Resistance Movement… There is no solution for the Palestinian question except through Jihad. Initiatives, proposals, and international conferences are all a waste of time and vain endeavors.[88]

This attitude is not limited to the militant Hamas. It is echoed throughout the Palestinian curriculum. Here is a translation of the Palestinian national anthem taught to schoolchildren in third-grade[89]:

Fida'i[a], Fida'i, Fida'i,

Oh my land, the land of my ancestors

Fida'i, Fida'i, Fida'i,

Oh my people, people of Eternity

With my determination, my fire and the volcano of my revenge

With the longing of my blood for my land and my home

I have climbed the mountains and fought the struggle

---

[a] The word *fida'i* can be translated in multiple ways. It can be understood as "the object of my sacrifice," but it can also be understood as "guerrilla suicide commando." This poem utilizes a play on words to convey both interpretations.

I have conquered the impossible and smashed the bonds

Fida'i, Fida'i, Fida'i,

Oh my land, the land of my ancestors

Fida'i, Fida'i, Fida'i,

Oh my people, people of Eternity

With the wind's resolve and the weapon's fire

And the determination of my people to fight the struggle

Palestine is my home and the trail of my victory

Palestine is my revenge and the land of steadfastness

Fida'i, Fida'i, Fida'i,

Oh my land, the land of my ancestors

Fida'i, Fida'i, Fida'i,

Oh my people, people of Eternity

By the oath under the flag

By my land and my people and the fire of pain

I will live as a Fida'i, and I will remain a Fida'i

And I will die as a Fida'i – until my country returns

Fida'i, Fida'i, Fida'i,

Oh my land, the land of my ancestors

Fida'i, Fida'i, Fida'i,

Oh my people, people of Eternity

Another example from the Palestinian curriculum is the following poem taught to third graders, entitled "Land of the Generous":

I vow I shall sacrifice my blood to saturate
the land of the generous

And eliminate the usurper from my country
and annihilate the remnants of the foreigners.[90]

Even arithmetic is taught by using the number of martyrs in the first and second Intifada and the number of Palestinians in Israeli prisons.[a][91][92]

---

[a] On a side note, teaching basic arithmetic through the language of violence did not originate with the Palestinians – the CIA actually beat them to it decades earlier. When the United States was still supporting the Taliban in their fight

These are not cherry-picked examples. A report by Eldad Pardo from the Hebrew University of Jerusalem lists many more examples from the Palestinian school curriculum that glorify violence, instilling into students the *dangerous narrative* that that is the only solution to the plight of the Palestinians.

Even children's programs on Palestinian television incite violence. The rhetoric of one show, called *Tomorrow's Pioneers*, was so appalling, it was surreal. It was like Sesame Street, if Sesame Street were directed by Joseph Goebbels. The show has since been canceled, but nevertheless it lasted for four seasons. Here is a transcript of a typical conversation from that show that took place between the child host Saraa, the bumblebee-costumed co-host Nahul[a], and their guests – two girls not older than eight.

---

against the Russians, they didn't just provide them with military hardware, they also provided them with school textbooks produced by an American university that taught math problems with variables like "Russian infidels killed" and "bullets used."

[a] Nahul is the co-host in season two. In the first season, the co-host was Nahul's cousin, Farfour the mouse. In that year's season finale, Farfour was shown being beaten to death by an actor posing as an Israeli official. Nahul himself dies in the second season when Israeli authorities block him from reaching a hospital. He is succeeded by Assoud the rabbit who, you see the pattern here, also dies at the hands of the Israeli at the end of season three during an Israeli military strike.

Saraa: *What does a policeman do?*

Nahul: *He catches thieves, and he solves problems…*

Saraa: *… and he kills Jews, right?*

Guest: *Yes.*

Saraa: *You want to be like him?*

Guest: (*Girl nods.*)

Saraa: *God willing, when you grow up…*

Girl: *So that I can shoot Jews.*

Saraa (excitedly): *All of them? All of them?*

Girl: *Yes.*

Saraa: *Good.*[93]

Now to be clear, as far as children's programs are concerned, that show falls on the extreme end of the spectrum. Never in my childhood did I encounter anything similar to it. So, it is not representative of kids' shows throughout the Muslim world. Also, I do not believe the opinions expressed on that show represent how Muslims think. But here is the problem: the *dangerous narratives* that the show drew from – narratives that give primacy to violence and liberation over achievement – are indeed prevalent. If it were not so, that program would not have lasted a single episode, much less four seasons.

How many more decades have to be squandered before Muslims realize that this attitude is folly? How long will it take Muslims to realize that armed struggle in Palestine and the rest of the Arab world, in all its forms, is a Sisyphean endeavor? It will not end the plight of the Palestinians. Neither will it bring them justice. It will only consume resources that would be better spent improving the lives of people in this region.

And yet Palestinians and Muslims continue pushing their "Jihad is the solution" narrative. Manpower and resources are poured into primitive homemade Qassam rockets, worth $800 a pop.[94] Ingenuity is reserved for finding new ways to start forest fires with flaming kites and – I kid you not – helium inflated burning condoms![95]

Freedom, Democracy, Justice, and Renaissance brought to you by Durex, the jihadi's number one choice for inflatable burning condoms.[a]

---

[a] Perhaps Hamas should adopt a new emblem: a giant flaming condom.

This is what Muslims have reduced themselves to: pinning their hopes and dreams for civilization on a papa-stopper.

Lobbing catapulty projectiles, not knowing where they will land and starting forest fires, is inexcusable from a moral perspective. There is no justification for firing a rocket knowing full well it could land in the middle of a school yard during recess. Even if we were to discount the moral perspective and look at the issue as a purely utilitarian one, we see that these attacks are counterproductive as well. They make Palestinians lose their moral high-ground. It places them in a moral quagmire where both sides are in some way at fault, thereby undermining their own image in the international community. Moreover, it undermines the efforts of Israeli dissidents and moderates who oppose the unjust policies of their regime, and it herds everyone into the camps of the unscrupulous, the hardliners, and the fanatics.

Even attacks on military targets and checkpoints are counterproductive. An attack on Israeli soldiers – whether by mortar, knife, or slingshot – is not going to further the Palestinian cause. A common refrain is that Palestinians have the right to be angry. Granted, but expressing their anger in a violent manner sustains and exacerbates the very conditions that draw their ire in the first place. It provokes more repression, and it serves to perpetuate the endless cycle of violence in which the Palestinians themselves receive the lion's share of the suffering.

Albert Einstein once said that insanity was doing the same thing over and over again and expecting different results. Palestinians have been doing just that, and there is no method to their madness. They need to approach this issue in another manner. I propose an eight-step program to secure the rights of Palestinians and improve their situation.

One, disband Hamas, Fatah, and any military or paramilitary organization that fancies itself a "resistance" group. Replace them with civilian technocratic institutions that would use legitimate economic and political means to improve conditions for the Palestinians.

Two, complete disarmament. Hand in all weapons and ammunition to an international organization. Rockets, mortars, anti-tank weapons, grenades, guns of all sorts, and even slingshots should all be relinquished.[a] The narrative of armed resistance should be done with.

---

[a] Even for policemen. They can carry batons; no need for guns. Only a small multinational peacekeeping force would have access to weapons, and their purpose would be strictly to deter the formation of new rebel movements and guarantee internal security.

Three, focus on rebuilding and education. Instead of throwing stones, stack them. Build schools, universities, hospitals. Build proper homes and proper streets. Plant trees instead of burning them.

Four, ditch the *al-Nakba* narrative. No more sob stories for something that happened nearly seventy years ago. Throughout history, millions were forcibly expelled from their homes and there was no enduring refugee problem. Turkey displaced more than a million Greeks; Greece displaced half a million Turks.[96] Russia displaced more than a million Poles. Poland, Czechoslovakia, Hungary, Romania, and Yugoslavia displaced fourteen million Germans. India displaced more than five million Muslims. Pakistan displaced more than five million Hindus and Sikhs. Algeria displaced a million Pied-Noir French.[97] And China recently displaced one and a half million of its own citizens just to build a dam.[98] They all managed to move on. Time for the Palestinians to move on too and build a constructive identity that does not revolve around various concepts of violent struggle.

Five, endure in peace, though bitter it will be at first, just as Germany endured history's most terrifying peace. In a generation, the stability and prosperity that come with peace will create an environment that is more conducive to securing everyone's rights.

Six, stop painting Israel as evil incarnate. Some time ago, I was having a conversation about this, arguing that Israel is not as bad as Muslims commonly portray it. The rebuttal was: "But what about Ahed Tamimi?"

Ahed Tamimi, the Palestinian teenager with hair like Princess Merida from the Disney movie *Brave*, had recently become the poster child of the Palestinian resistance. She had achieved that status after a video showing her slapping an Israeli soldier went viral – an incident that she was consequently jailed for by Israeli authorities.

To put things into perspective, further background information is required for this story. Ahed was not an insolent girl acting out with no good reason. That video showing her slapping an Israeli soldier happened after her fifteen-year-old cousin was shot in the head at close range and heinously disfigured for life.

Ahed Tamimi's case does indeed demonstrate ongoing Israeli oppression, as those who bring up her case want the world to see. But to be fair, it also represents something else, something that Muslims find hard to acknowledge, much less admit. It represents Israeli restraint.

A state in which a teenage girl can slap a soldier and suffer no horrible consequences is not the epitome of evil. Ahed came out of the jail smiling gleefully with no indication that she had been subjected to any cruelty or abuse whilst in prison. Can you imagine a blonde sixteen-year-old girl coming out of jail smiling as such if she were just leaving an Egyptian prison, or a Syrian one, or a Saudi one?

Sure, there is a lot that Israel is accountable for, especially regarding its past and ongoing crimes against the Palestinians. After all, this is a regime which, by the UN Council's admission, does not shy away from shooting children. [99] One need only read Max Blumenthal's eye-opening book *Goliath: Life and Loathing in Greater Israel* to realize the full measure of their transgressions. But at the end of the day, Israeli crimes are dwarfed by the injustices of so-called "Muslim regimes" against their own citizens. I am not absolving Israel of its crimes, but as a Muslim I am sick of Israel being the object of Muslim angst while Muslim countries get a free pass as they oppress their own people. When it comes to infringing the human rights of Muslims, Muslim countries have a record far worse than Israel's. Health care, education, and services are all woefully substandard in Muslim countries, and decent economic opportunities are scarce. In Egypt, poverty is so harsh that even bread is made in two types: decent bread for the rich and low quality bread for the poor. Some countries like Saudi Arabia, Kuwait, Qatar, and the UAE do enjoy economic prosperity but only because they are hogging the natural resources in this region for themselves. Qatar, for example, has just over three hundred thousand citizens but has monopolized 13 percent of the world's reserves in natural gas for itself.[100] That is how their decrepit, sinecure-filled state has a GDP per capita higher than Luxembourg's. Meanwhile, right across the Red Sea, Muslims in Somalia are left to starve even though Muhammad warned that, "Whenever people anywhere allow a man to go hungry, they are outside the protection of Allah."

But let us brush aside the injustices perpetrated by Muslim countries against their own people for now. How do Palestinian refugees fare in those countries? Are they treated well? Do they enjoy equal rights?

No.

In fact, while Muslim countries lament the conditions of the Palestinians in Israel, they mistreat the Palestinians in their own countries. For seventy years, many Palestinians have been made to live in overcrowded squalid refugee camps resembling ghettos and shanty towns. In most cases, they are not given citizenship. In some countries, they are not even given the right to own property, send their kids to local schools, or even get work permits.[101] This is done on the cynical pretense that if they were to be treated like decent human beings, they would integrate in their host countries, and then would not go back home. Thus it would be tantamount to helping "the usurping Zionist entity"[a] in their plan to occupy Palestine. So making Palestinians live in wretched conditions, denying them social and economic rights, and keeping them preoccupied with basic survival is all done in the oh-so-noble spirit of helping maintain their desire to return to Palestine.

---

[a] "The usurping Zionist entity" is a common epithet used in the Arab world to refer to Israel. Edward Said, the late Palestinian public intellectual and professor at Columbia University, has described the phrase's use by Arabs as a "foolish and wasteful policy" as it reflects a refusal to analyze Israel and Israelis.

But at least they were not expelled from their homes, like they were in Palestine. At least Muslim countries do not demolish Palestinian homes the way Israel does, right?

Wrong again.

In the 1950s, Iraq and Saudi Arabia expelled Palestinian workers who went on strike. In 1970, Jordan expelled twenty thousand Palestinians and demolished their homes.[102] In 1994, Libya expelled up to thirty thousand Palestinians.[103]

But the examples above all pale in comparison to what happened in yet another Muslim state. In 1991, the Palestinian Liberation Organization (PLO) endorsed Iraq's invasion of Kuwait. As a form of collective punishment, Kuwait expelled *two hundred thousand* Palestinians, who had been living there for decades and had nothing to do with the PLO, "in a systematic campaign of terror, violence, and economic pressure." In addition, Kuwait denied another *two hundred thousand* Palestinians the right of return after they had fled the country during Saddam's invasion of Kuwait.[104]

According to American academic Laurie Brand, Palestinians had helped shape Kuwait's social, economic, and political development more than any other expatriate group. Not that it mattered to the ingrate Kuwaitis. After Kuwait's ethnic cleansing, Palestinians, who used to constitute 18.7 percent of the population in that country in 1990, made up only 0.01 percent of the population in 1995. And of the enormous 33 billion dollars lost by the evicted Palestinians, only a measly 4.4 percent was compensated.[a][105]

Taking all of this into consideration, I think it is high time for Muslims to reorient their discontent towards their own regimes. They need to deal with the rot within before crying foul that something is rotten in the state of Denmark – or in this case, Israel.

Seven, establish lines of communications with Israel. Open Israeli embassies in the Muslim world so that ordinary Muslims and Israelis can work together to create interpersonal ties where none existed before. Undertake joint initiatives and research projects. Set up programs between universities to exchange students and professors. Open the door for increased fruitful interaction between Muslims and Israelis. The idea behind this is not to

---

[a] In a display of flagrant hypocrisy, on December 1992, a year after they had expelled 400,000 Palestinians, Kuwait sent a delegation to Lebanon to condemn Israel for deporting four Palestinians and took the opportunity to boast of their solidarity with Palestinian refugees. Kuwait, thy name is chutzpah!

acquiesce to unjust policies by the State of Israel but to prevent it from spiraling further into religious Zionism. This is critical, because as Israeli screenwriter Kobi Niv pointed out in *Haaretz*, there is an ongoing battle at the moment between the religious-Zionist wing and the liberal-secular wing in Israel for the soul of the Jewish Israeli people, and the former are clearly winning.[106] I believe, if Muslims cease their uncompromising rhetoric and engage positively with Israelis, they can undermine the narratives of the religious-Zionists that paint Muslims as the villainous "other" and tip the scales in favor of the liberal-secular wing. Consequently, Muslims can turn Israel from a nuclear-powered enemy in their heartland into an ally bound together by a mutual defense agreement. Muhammad himself entered into a similar arrangement with the Jews of Medina after he fled Mecca. This is evident in the famous Charter of Medina.[a] So if the Prophet did it, why can't we?

Finally moving on to point number eight, accept that the solutions will be imperfect. Stop teaching school children that "the Palestinian flag will be hoisted on the

---

[a] The fact that the Jewish tribes in Medina later broke the treaty they had with the Muslims and allied themselves with their enemies does not detract from the lawfulness of entering into such an arrangement in the first place.

city's walls after the liberation from Israeli occupation"[a] and that they will "inevitably return."[107] Stop using fictitious maps of Palestine in school textbooks that do not include Israel.

Solutions which involve Palestinians reclaiming all the land that was taken from them are fantasies detached from realities on the ground. Expecting a return of all seven million Palestinians living abroad is absurd for the same reasons. *Realpolitik* dictates that it is not going to happen. These narratives only serve to promote self-delusion and bar the way to any conclusive peace agreement.

Attainable goals would be the following: an end to the system of apartheid inside Israel. No more settler-only roads. No more refusing to issue building permits to Palestinians. No more setting up ad hoc checkpoints and blocking access to places of worship, employment, agricultural lands, schools, and hospitals. No more giving free rein to fundamentalist settlers to attack Palestinians. No more restrictions on non-military goods going into Gaza and the Palestinian territories.

---

[a] Notice the medieval imagery in this sentence. This goes back to Muslims' fixation on the period of early Islamic conquests. The author of the school textbook – and by extension the students who study with it – see the Palestinian problem through the prism of that time period. This prevents them from coming to grips with reality and approaching this thorny issue in a manner that takes into account its actual complexity.

As for the Palestinians living abroad, a system of reparations can be put in place to help them integrate into the societies that they have been living in for over seven decades.

These are actionable steps that could improve the Palestinians' lot. By extension, the Muslim world would finally no longer be hung up on the Palestinian issue and could then focus on internal development. That is what Muslims need right now. They do not need liberty. Liberty is inconsequential in determining quality of life if you are busy holding camel beauty contests[a] and injecting camels with Botox to enhance their "natural beauty."[108]

Muslims call for the liberation of Palestine, but they never stop to pause and think what kind of state Palestine would be if it were an independent state with sovereignty over all the land it lays claim to. Would it be a society with Nordic-style social egalitarianism and development? Would it even be as good to its citizens as Israel is towards Jewish Israelis? No, of course not. It would be nothing more than a petty Middle Eastern fiefdom mired with social and economic inequality and ruled over by a corrupt,

---

[a] Sadly this is not a joke. Saudi Arabia actually holds a camel beauty pageant called the "King Abdulaziz Camel Festival" where total prize money is roughly 32 million dollars. Oh and if you're wondering, yes they hold goat beauty pageants too.

ineffective ruling class who are solely concerned with lining their pockets – just like every sovereign Muslim majority state from the Persian Gulf to the Atlantic.

The "Free Palestine" movement is in some ways not so different from the independence movements in the Middle East that sought to break away from colonial powers post World War I. These states got their independence. Lebanon, Syria, Iraq, Egypt, Libya, Algeria are all "free" now, and what a glorious freedom that has been. Lacking in both basic human rights and economic opportunity, and plagued by sectarian violence and civil strife, these states offer little more to their citizens than an oppressive security apparatus to keep them in line.

All these countries celebrate their "independence day," whereas in fact they should lament it. An "independence day" should be commemorated as a day of national tragedy. In colonial times, those states demonstrated their municipal pride. Their roads were well maintained, and their schools, hospitals, and public institutions ran efficiently. They thrived.

Now to be clear, this is not an apologia for colonialism per se. I am not discounting the fact that colonialism can indeed be repressive and that it does benefit colonial rulers more than it does the natives, especially in the short term. But using force to break away from a larger political entity is usually not conducive to better conditions. Even when the break is successful, the locals are worse off, because the new state is unable to provide the same measure of political and economic stability as the regime it replaces.

Take Lebanon for example. A hundred years ago under the Ottoman Empire, Lebanon enjoyed a railway system. Now more than a century later, it doesn't. Instead it has filthy congested streets, daily electricity cuts, a poor infrastructure, a debt-ridden economy, and a floundering currency. Sure, the Lebanese flag has its own spot in the long row fronting the United Nations General Assembly on Manhattan's First Avenue, but what of it? That conveys neither equal esteem nor equal success to the other nations whose flags are hoisted abreast ours; to think otherwise is self-aggrandizement.

The picture becomes even more dismal when we factor in the tragic toll of the Lebanese civil war. One hundred twenty thousand killed and countless raped, in a country of just three million people. Had Lebanon remained part of the Ottoman Empire or France, those people would still be alive. If only the Lebanese had not substituted the *Reşadiye Marşı* or *La Marseillaise* for a soppy, milquetoast, and plagiarized tune.[a] All the senseless suffering and destruction, for which the Lebanese pay for to this very day, would have been averted.

Lebanon is not an isolated case. The same case could be made for Syria, Iraq, Libya, Sudan, or any of the new make-believe modern nation states that popped up after the unfortunate demise of colonialism.

The notion of prosperity and justice through "independence" is a chimera. This is even more true when a nation's culture is philistine and primitive and its society is in tatters – as is the case in most of the Muslim world. Under such conditions, independence[b] does not improve the situation in the "liberated" nation. Take a look at Iraq. What was the first thing hundreds of thousands of Iraqi Shiite did upon the liberation of their country and the downfall of Saddam Hussein? They took to the streets and flagellated themselves.[109] While fresh water and electricity were scarce, and while schools, hospitals, museums, and

---

[a] Yes, it recently came to light that the Lebanese national anthem is not in fact Lebanese. The tune and even parts of the lyrics were plagiarized from the national anthem of a short-lived state that existed in the 1920s in northern Morocco called the Republic of the Rif.

[b] "Independence" (i.e. the transfer of power from foreign overlords to local ones).

public institutions were being looted, these "pilgrims" went about chanting and cutting themselves. As political theorist Edmund Burke put it, liberty without wisdom and virtue is "folly."[110]

So hanging onto the current *dangerous narrative* whereby salvation rests on the liberation of Palestine in the aftermath of a great apocalyptic conflict in which stones and trees start to speak[a] will only ensure further suffering for both the Palestinians and the rest of the Muslim world.

The poet Dylan Thomas wrote, "Rage, rage against the dying of the light." That is how Arabs and Palestinians have been living over the past 70 years. I say it is time to stop, and light a goddamn candle instead.

---

[a] This refers to a prophecy in Islamic eschatology about a battle in the End Times between Jews and Muslims. It states that stones and trees will speak to aid the Muslims in battle. One tree, however, the *Gharqad* (Boxthorn) tree, will be mute.

Chapter 5

Of Wealth and Social Mores

The West is prosperous. They are more technologically advanced than us. Their scientific discoveries have no equal in our society. They have hoisted their flag on the moon, and someday soon, they will do the same on Mars.

They may be the masters of this world, but we are the aristocracy in the dominion of God. We are more spiritual than they are, and we have retained our moral values and our humanity. They can never rival us in that.

That is what most Muslims tell themselves anyway.

It is not that we spurn wealth. No, if the conspicuous consumption of wealthy Arabs is any indication, we do care a great deal about it. In the Gospel of Matthew, Christians are told that "it is easier for a camel to go through the eye of a needle than for someone who is rich to enter the kingdom of

God." There is no analogous verse in the Quran. So Muslims are quite comfortable with enormous amounts of personal wealth.

However, whereas Muslims covet wealth at a personal level, they spurn it at a societal level. We do not think much of the wealth of other nations; it does not command a prominent position in our collective consciousness. We do not dream of better cities, of greener spaces, of cleaner air, of meaningful jobs. No, on a national level, we only dream of our militaristic power dynamics vis-à-vis other countries.

Maybe that is one of the reasons there is no science-fiction genre in the Muslim world. Take a show like *Star Trek: The Next Generation* where society has attained an unprecedented level of prosperity and comfort through peace and cooperation. Muslims would never produce a show like that. In fact, the very idea of them coming up with that premise sounds absurd. First, it would entail seeing themselves as part of a greater humanity rather than a distinct group. Second, themes of peace, well-being, and technological advancement are nowhere near as appealing to Muslims as the themes of power and status.

That is why period dramas are very popular in the Muslim World. Turkish historical television shows like

Magnificent Century and *Diriliş: Ertuğrul* captivate audiences not just in Turkey where they are produced but in the rest of the Muslim world as well. These shows deliver what Muslims seek. They portray Muslims as a distinct group engaged in a power struggle with the world. And while they do revel in Muslims' prosperity at that time, it is a prosperity attained by military might. All the events in these shows are seen through the prism of power.

I believe this *dangerous narrative* that scorns development in favor of power dynamics is a modern one. As we lagged behind the world materially, we convinced ourselves that peaceful prosperity is not something important after all. In an effort to protect our frail psyches, we have diminished in our eyes that which we are unable to attain.

Regardless of its origins, this narrative compels Muslims to view material wealth and spiritual wealth as two dichotomous spheres. They argue that a society's health is determined purely by its spirituality, values, and moral conduct. From a Muslim's perspective, these in turn are derived solely from religion.

If it were so, however, why has Western Europe of all places, managed to create such an equitable society? They who have retained so little of their religious heritage, they who have abandoned their churches, were still able to turn Europe into The Land of Cockaigne.

I posit the following explanation: there is actually a close connection between material and cultural values. Whereas a society's material wealth does not fully determine its social mores, it does have an ennobling effect on them, especially on a macro level.

A prosperous society is more likely to look after its own by virtue of being able to do so. On the other hand, a society in which everyone is scurrying after their daily bread pays little heed to the well-being of its citizens.

Recently, France enacted a law which has been dubbed "the right to disconnect."[111] It rules that employees are not obliged to answer any work-related email or phone call outside working hours. Can you imagine a law like that coming from Egypt, or Bangladesh, or Turkey? No, only a wealthy society thinks like that.

It is no coincidence that all labor laws protecting workers from exploitation by their employers, from the five-day work week to the minimum wage, were conceptualized and implemented first in countries already enjoying a degree of prosperity.

Even at a micro level prosperity improves interpersonal relationships. People are more likely to be kinder when they are not in a desperate struggle for survival. For example, Germans have shown a great deal of compassion and humanity in recent years in assisting Syrian refugees and migrants, whereas Turks are often heard grumbling about them. The disparity in attitude does not stem from an inherent quality in the character of Germans or Turks. It stems from the socioeconomic conditions that citizens face in those countries. When people are trying to make ends meet, as they are in Turkey, they are much less likely to exhibit munificence.

And people are not only kinder when they are better off, they are smarter too. Research has shown that just being in a stressful financial situation lowers a person's IQ by 14 points.[112]

Material wealth at a societal level is not the sole determinant of our social mores, but it lends itself to the establishment of a kinder society. It is good that we have retained our belief in the transcendent and that we look at ourselves within the framework of eternity. But in spurning material wealth in this world, we desert the means to establish a humane society. And in deserting the means, we desert the ends.

Chapter 6
Bombs and Bombast

On the eve of the Arab-Israeli War of 1948, Musa Alami, a prominent politician, toured the Middle East to speak with the leaders of the Arab world. The top officials in every country he visited reassured him that victory was in the bag. In Damascus, the President of Syria even divulged a surprising military secret: "I can tell you in confidence that we even have an atomic bomb... Yes, it was made locally; we fortunately found a very clever fellow, a tinsmith...”[113]

Of course, Syria possessed no atomic bomb, locally manufactured or otherwise. Previous attestations of their own combat readiness were also grossly exaggerated. While Jewish militias possessed B-17 Flying Fortresses and M4 Sherman tanks[114], Yemen and Saudi Arabia dispatched battalions armed with knives and scimitars to protect the

Holy Land.[115] Moreover, the maps that the Arab military high command relied on were more than thirty years out of date. Arab armies spent their time wandering aimlessly all over the Holy Land. Studying their troop movements in that war brings to mind *The Benny Hill Show* theme song.

The Arabs suffered a humiliating defeat in the War of 1948, a result you would never have thought possible if you were to form your opinion based on the Arab rhetoric that preceded it.

A similar incident took place during the 2003 U.S.-led invasion of Iraq. Even as U.S. forces pushed deeper into Iraqi territory, the Iraqi information minister, Mohammad Saeed al-Sahaf (better known to American viewers as "Baghdad Bob" or "Comical Ali"), kept making outlandish pronouncements of Iraqi military supremacy. Here are some quotes from his speeches:

> They're not even [within] 100 miles [of Baghdad]. They are not in any place. They hold no place in Iraq. This is an illusion ... they are trying to sell to the others an illusion.

They fled. The American louts fled. Indeed, concerning the fighting waged by the heroes of the Arab Socialist Baath Party yesterday, one amazing thing really is the cowardice of the American soldiers. We had not anticipated this.

We're giving them a real lesson today. Heavy doesn't accurately describe the level of casualties we have inflicted.

We defeated them yesterday. God willing, I will provide you with more information. I swear by God, I swear by God, those who are staying in Washington and London have thrown these mercenaries in a crematorium.[116]

He continued to make proclamations of victory even as American forces entered Baghdad and were just a few hundred meters away from his press conference. Reality had no effect on tempering his outlandish claims. As long as he had a platform, absurdities and exaggerations kept pouring out of his mouth *ad captandum vulgus*.

A more recent demonstration of this pattern played itself out in the aftermath of the assassination of Iranian General Qassem Soleimani by an American drone strike in 2020.

In the wake of the assassination, vows of revenge reached a fever pitch in Iranian media. Iran's supreme leader himself, Grand Ayatollah Ali Khamenei, tweeted that "severe revenge" awaited the Americans. High officials in the Iranian military upped the ante, promising "the expulsion of the Americans from the region."[117] These declarations must have been very pleasing to the crowds chanting "Death to America" in the streets, but what ultimately happened?

Nothing. Iran fired missiles near Iraqi bases, which resulted in a grand total of zero American casualties, then proclaimed that General Soleimani had been avenged.[a]

These are not isolated cases. Examples of bombast and flamboyant declarations abound in this part of the world. Though this problem is most pronounced in the

---

[a] Of course, Iranian media didn't admit right away that their sworn enemies had suffered no casualties. Initial reports by Iranian media claimed dozens killed and hundreds injured. Even later when they could no longer maintain those lies, they stuck to the narrative that it was a "great" and "earth-shattering" military strike.

realm of politics, it can also be encountered in normal daily discourse. In a viral video I saw recently, a Lebanese man was asking a woman's parents for her hand in marriage on behalf of his son. He told the father of the bride-to-be that if one were to use all the water in the oceans as ink, it would not be enough to write about the virtues of his family. In another instance, a drifter doing odd jobs and living beneath the poverty line once told me, "if you're looking for me, just ask around for 'The Emperor.' Everybody in the neighborhood knows me."

I have lived for some time in both Canada and Ireland, and I could never imagine someone there making similar statements outside the confines of a mental institution. In the Muslim world, however, such proclamations of grandeur are commonplace, even though they are often in stark contrast with reality.

Much has been said about hyperbole in this part of the world. One of the popular explanations offered for this phenomenon is that it has to do with the influence of the Arabic language. In the Arab world, the classical Arabic used for writing and official purposes is not the same as the spoken Arabic used in daily speech. The difference in vocabulary, grammar, sentence structure, and pronunciation between the two is so extensive that they are almost different languages. It has been proposed that this dichotomy between written language and spoken language creates a duality in the Arab character which in turn feeds into this mythomania.

Maybe so, but I disagree with the common conclusion that, for Arabs, words are more important than actions. I think a better explanation is that in this part of the world, people do not describe the world as it is but rather how they would like it to be, mainly to save face. In the personal examples I mentioned earlier, this was all implicitly understood by the parties involved. There was no malice.

The absence of malice, however, does not make it benign. The idea that truth is subservient to image or face-saving is a *dangerous narrative*.

Saving face at the expense of truth can have disastrous consequences when it is unclear when one is speaking the truth and when one is exaggerating. When Hamas or Hezbollah or the Egyptian army falsely present themselves as formidable forces capable of standing up to Israel's military might, they deceive people in this part of the world into believing that a confrontational stance could be in their favor. This, of course, is far from the truth.

Israel's army is twice the size of the French and British armies combined. Furthermore, it can call up, equip, and deploy thousands of reservists in less than twenty-four hours. [118] If pressed, Israel can fight on all fronts concurrently – and not only hold its own but devastate and overrun all neighboring countries. When Hezbollah "stood up" to Israel during the 2006 Israel-Hezbollah War, it was not because Hezbollah was strong – it was because Israel was concerned, to some extent, about civilian casualties. They did not want the international community to mobilize against them. Had Israel been indifferent to international opprobrium, and therefore unconcerned with restraint, Hezbollah would not have stood a chance.

When Lebanese people present their country as "the Switzerland of the East" while its rubbish is heaped on the streets and its mountains are defaced with excessive quarrying, such a statement is not ameliorative, it is delusional.

When people lose sight of reality, they lose the ability to affect it, because the first step to get out of a quandary is to see the quandary. It is like the case of a junkie. As long as he is tripping, he is not going to realize the destitution he is in and consequently will not take measures to change his life.

In the *hadith*, we are told the story of man who went to Muhammad complaining that there were too many rules in Islam. The man said he could not abide by them all and asked the Prophet to give him just one rule to live by. The Prophet obliged him with a two word answer: "Don't lie." If only Muslims lived by that rule.

Chapter 7

The Turbaned Thinker Toppled

On the fourth question, the contestant was stumped.

It was on a recent episode of the Turkish version of the show *Who Wants to Be a Millionaire*. The multiple choice question that mystified the twenty-six-year-old economics graduate was: in which country is the Great Wall of China?

At a loss, the contestant turned to the audience for help. They did not fare that much better than her. Forty-nine percent of the audience got the answer wrong![119]

How did we get to the point where out of a hundred people, almost half of them cannot figure out that the Great Wall of China is in China?

Here are some sobering statistics that could shed light on this mystery.

Every year, Greece translates more books from English than the entire Arab world translates in five years.[120]

Think this is bad?

Spain translates more books into Spanish in one year than the entire Arab world has translated into Arabic since the 9th century.[121]

If we look at books published, the statics are equally disheartening. In the Arab world, the number of books published in Arabic annually is about 5 percent of the overall number of books published in the United States.[122] And that is without getting into the quality of the books published, as most books written in the Arab world tend to be derivative and of dubious merit.

As for Muslim Nobel Laureates in sciences, since the beginning of the 20th century, there have only been three – one Turkish, one Pakistani, and one Arab!

It was not always like that. Israeli scholar Martin Kramer notes, "Had there been Nobel Prizes in 1000, they would have gone almost exclusively to Muslims."[123] At that time, the famous library of Cordoba contained 400,000 volumes – quite possibly more books than all of Western Europe had at that time.[124] Back then, the construction of universities and colleges was a passion for Muslims.[125] So was intellectual inquiry. An article in the *New York Times* states:

> Commanded by the Quran to seek knowledge and read nature for signs of the creator and inspired by a treasure trove of ancient Greek learning, Muslims created a society that in the Middle Ages was the scientific center of the world. The Arabic language was synonymous with learning and science for 500 years, a golden age that can count among its credits the precursors to modern universities, algebra… and even the notion of science as an empirical inquiry.[126]

Neil deGrasse Tyson noted in one of his lectures that two thirds of all the stars that have names are named in Arabic because Muslim Arabs were pioneers in that field.[127]

Muslims today take great vicarious pride in the intellectual achievements of their forefathers. But one thing is clear: those days of scintillating intellectualism are long gone.[a][128] The Muslim intellectual landscape today is a barren and benighted wasteland.

In such an environment, it is unsurprising to discover some anti-intellectual *dangerous narratives*. This chapter explores three types of anti-intellectual narratives in the Muslim world. Let's start with anti-intellectual narratives regarding science.

There are a number of anti-intellectual narratives floating around in the Muslim world which are spread by preachers with no grounding in science.[b][129] Most of these narratives, however, do not hold much sway in the Muslim world bar one – creationism.

---

[a] The reason behind the ossification of the Muslim mind is explored in great detail in Robert R. Reilly's excellent book, *The Closing Of The Muslim Mind*. According to Reilly, this is rooted in an intellectual crisis that took place around the turn of the first millennium between two schools of thought in Islam, the *Ash'arites* and the *Mu'tazalites*. Though they flourished for some time, the *Mu'tazalites*, who emphasized the primacy of reason, were ultimately defeated and suppressed by the *Ash'arites*, who emphasized the primacy of dogma and blind faith. Had the *Mu'tazalite* position won the battle of ideas, it's quite possible that the Muslim world would not have deteriorated to the state it is in now. In fact, given that the Muslim world had a head start, it is quite plausible that they would have retained their edge over the West – and the rest of the world.

[b] For example, Ibn Baz, former grand mufti of Saudi Arabia from 1993 until his death in 1999, rejected the Copernican system. In his book, he states that the sun revolves around the earth. He also states that the earth is flat and declares that all those who believe otherwise are apostates.

The majority of Muslims believe that evolution posits that humans descend from apes and that Charles Darwin was a nefarious charlatan.

Not to be outdone, the Muslim community produced its own champion for the creationist cause, Adnan Oktar. One part Pat Robertson and three parts Hugh Hefner, with a harem full of surgically-enhanced "kittens" and buff "lions," the Turkish Oktar produced an 870 glossy-paged *Atlas of Creation* that he mailed – unsolicited of course – to tens of thousands of schools and researchers around the world.

Unsurprisingly, the book, a collection of pseudo-scientific claims, failed to debunk anything. In his review of Oktar's magnum opus, Richard Dawkins commented, "I am at a loss to reconcile the expensive and glossy production values of this book with the breathtaking inanity of the content."[130]

Other figures more respectable than Oktar, like Indian medical doctor and preacher Zakir Naik, take a different approach. When asked about the theory of evolution by an ex-Muslim medical student during one of his lectures, he explained that the theory of evolution is unproven because it is a "theory" and not a fact. Naik brought down the house with that comment. The medical student, however, who was familiar with what the term "theory" actually means in science, remained unimpressed.[131]

The sad thing about this story is that the ex-Muslim who came up with the question told Naik that if he got a convincing answer, he would go back to being a Muslim. However, by clinging to anti-intellectual dogma and insisting on presenting Islam in a manner that goes counter to science, Naik lost him.

Ironically, support for the theory of evolution, which forms the basis of modern biology, can even be found in medieval Islamic scholarship. Nearly five-hundred years before Darwin, the renowned Arab Scholar Ibn Khaldun wrote in his book *The Muqaddimah*:

> One should then look at the world of creation. It started out from the minerals and progressed, in an ingenious, gradual manner, to plants and animals… The animal world then widens, its species become numerous, and, in a gradual process of creation, it finally leads to man, who is able to think and

reflect. The higher stage of man is reached from the world of the monkeys.[132]

Now, here is the kicker. Ibn Khaldun is not the only early Islamic source that proposes the theory of evolution. There is another source that precedes it by seven-hundred years: the Quran. As noted by US professor of physics, Dr. Serkan Zorba, the Quran itself lends support to this theory.[133] The Quran asks Muslims to reflect: "What is the matter with you that you don't attribute to God [due] grandeur, when he has created you in stages?" (71:13–14)

The Arabic word used for "in stages" is *atwaran*. The root verb of this word is *tawwar* which means "to evolve," and its noun form *tatawwur* literally means "development" or "evolution."

And not only does the Quran present creation as a gradual process, it even provides the methodology required to prove it is indeed so. The Quran instructs Muslims to, "Travel through the earth and observe how he began creation. Then God will produce the subsequent creation. God has power over all things." (29: 19–20)

This is what Darwin did. He travelled aboard the HMS Beagle to some of the most exotic locales on Earth, like the Galapagos Islands, and he observed nature in painstaking detail.

Darwin, a Jewish naturalist, showed more fidelity to the Quran – and to the scientific rigor of medieval Islamic Scholars – than modern Islamic preachers. Alas, that is a point that most Muslims remain unaware of.

There have indeed been some encouraging developments on this issue in recent years. Muslim scholars with backgrounds in science like Usama Hasan in the UK[134] and Dr. Adnan Ibrahim in Austria have come out in favor of human evolution. However, by-and-large, the narrative of insta-creationism continues to be pushed. In the 18th century, Voltaire noted that "false miracles" and "absurd legends" "extinguish religion in men's hearts" and lead them to the following conclusion:

> The heads of my religion have deceived me, therefore there is no religion; it is better to cast oneself into the arms of nature than into those of error; I would rather depend on the law of nature than on the inventions of men.[135]

Today, earnest, rational young Muslims are being led to the same conclusion. Muslims are being lost in droves in defensc of the indefensible.

The second type of anti-intellectual narratives pertains to Muslims' scornful disregard of philosophical knowledge that did not originate within the Muslim community. Having gone to many Friday sermons throughout my youth, I do not recall a single time when an imam made a reference to a Greek or Western philosopher. Not once did an imam mention Plato, Aristotle, Cicero, Augustine, Dante, Machiavclli, Hobbes, Rousseau, Burke, or Locke. Every sermon referenced the same Islamic sources *ad nauseam*. There was no effort whatsoever to draw any insight or any conclusions from non-Muslim sources.

This is not just a reflection of what Muslim theology students are exposed to in Islamic seminaries. It goes deeper than that. There is a strong belief among mainstream Muslims that the Quran, the *Hadith*, and commentaries about them are self-sufficient on an epistemological level. It is a belief that one need not look at other sources of philosophical knowledge, and in fact doing so can only lead to the corruption of the truth.

I remember as a child watching a clip from an Arabic historical series that stuck in my mind ever since. In it, two villains discuss the translation of Greek classics into Arabic. The first remarks that in doing so, Muslims will have access to a repertoire of knowledge which will make them stronger. However, his companion – the more devious of the two – remarks that these books, rather than make Muslims stronger, will actually corrupt them.

When I was researching Sayyid Qutb, I found the same idea that I had encountered in that series decades earlier. According to Qutb, the apotheosis of the first generation of Muslims that set them apart from all those who came after was that the first generation had the privilege of having "only one source of guidance." Later generations were corrupted by Greek philosophy and knowledge, Persian legends, Jewish scripture, and Christian theology. For Qutb, the syncretism of Islam led to the downfall of Muslims.[136]

Qutb forgets that during that time when Muslims were imbibing the wisdom of their predecessors and translating every book they could lay their hands on, they were powerful and prosperous. The present nadir in which the Muslim world currently subsists was not ushered in by those with a thirst for knowledge but by those who have spurned it, believing they already know all that needs knowing. And this state persists because so many Muslims, like the late Qutb, are adamant about that *dangerous narrative*.

Finally, the third type of anti-intellectual narratives deals with Islamic jurisprudence. This type can be broken down into three sub-narratives.

The first one is looking at actions taken by paragons of early Islamic history with neither an understanding of the rationale, nor the context that prompted them to act one way or another.

To interpret the Quran or *hadith*, or any text for that matter, "one must have a methodology, and in that methodology there are jurisprudential, linguistic, philosophical, historical, and moral perspectives."[137] Early Muslims understood that. They understood that literalism, which can freeze the text out of its context and its overall message, is not honesty or fidelity to the truth but is, in fact, dangerous. They understood that the literal meaning is not synonymous with the correct one, and hence the apparent meaning of a *hadith* injunction – or even a Quranic one – could be completely restricted, if by applying it in a specific context one breaks the core values of Islam.[a] Unbeknownst to their modern coreligionists, early Muslims showed remarkable ingenuity and adaptability in that regard.

For example, all four schools of Islamic jurisprudence traditionally accepted the notion of a "hidden pregnancy" (*al-haml al kamin*), which is a pregnancy that can last up to two, three, or four years from the date of conception.[138][139] This is scientifically impossible, as any baby in utero for more than 43 weeks would die. Many modern commentators hear this and attribute it to people being stupid back then. I think that is a flippant explanation. The well-read and well-traveled scholars were neither naïve nor stupid. They must have been aware that pregnancy lasts 40 weeks give or take. The reason they acknowledged the legitimacy of "hidden pregnancy" must have been to give a woman who was promiscuous after the death of her husband or in his absence an opportunity for acquittal. They did not want a woman in that situation to get punished, and neither did they want her child to be brought

---

[a] It is important to note here that this was not done as an act of rebellion. It stemmed from the understanding that the Quran, just like any other book, has an inherent ambiguity due to the interpretive gulf between God and the reader. God's meaning is sometimes rendered dim and doubtful by the cloudy medium through which it is communicated.

up as a bastard. They did so because they understood that in Islam, mercy and forgiveness should take precedence over punishment.[a]

Another example, from the Quran itself this time, is the following oft-quoted verse:

> Men are in charge of women by [right of] what Allah has given one over the other and what they spend [for maintenance] from their wealth. So righteous women are devoutly obedient, guarding in [the husband's] absence what Allah would have them guard. But those [wives] from whom you fear arrogance - [first] advise them; [then if they persist], forsake them in bed; and [finally], strike them. But if they obey you [once more], seek no means against

---

[a] I just brought up this example to showcase how far early Muslims would go to come up with a merciful ruling. Despite their good intentions, however, I don't think it was the right way to go about it, as it laces perception with dangerous naïveté. A community that accepts such fabrications and "noble" lies is likely to drift into gullibility and become vulnerable to manipulation by all sorts of pied pipers. It shouldn't require suspension of disbelief in order to be able to give out a merciful ruling.

them. Indeed, Allah is ever exalted and grand.[a] (4:34)

I will not go into the various other ways this verse can be translated from Arabic (for more on this, check the footnotes). The point is that even the Islamic scholars who understood the verse in line with the translation above – as many indeed did – never used it to condone violence against women. On the contrary, as Jonathan Brown, points out, "The most salient theme in the ulama's [Islamic scholars] writings across the centuries has been one of restricting almost completely the apparent meaning of this particular verse."[140] In other words, they appended this verse through exegesis to the point where it was no longer operative. Their reason for doing so stemmed from both their knowledge of the Prophet's life, which shows that Muhammad was averse to domestic violence and never hit a woman, and from their understanding that Islam's overarching and abiding objectives are affection and mercy.

---

[a] The translation I offered above is a common translation, but it's not the only one. As noted by Reza Aslan, this same verse could also be *literally* translated word for word in a manner which is completely different. "Men are the support of women as God gives some more means than others, and because they spend of their wealth (to provide for them)… As for women you feel are averse, talk to them suasively; then leave them alone in bed, turn away from them." One can hardly believe that this is a literal word-for-word translation of the same verse, but it is indeed so.

These days, however, parochial Islamic scholars, are obsessed with precedent and the letter of law, but show a complete lack of understanding – and even disregard – of its spirit.

The situations Muslims face in the 21st century do not always have parallels in 7th century Arabia. But that is alright. Islam is an organic religion; it was meant for all humanity and for all ages. However, in order to tap into that dynamism, one needs a solid understanding of the principals of Islam, not just its traditions. But most modern Islamic scholars do not get that. Instead, they try to strangle modernity wherever they find it. They regurgitate previous Muslim thinkers vacuously, without understanding the social and cultural milieu of those thinkers. Thinking of them, one is reminded of this famous line from Plato's Phaedrus: "They will be hearers of many things and will have learned nothing; they will appear to be omniscient and will generally know nothing; they will be tiresome, having the reputation of knowledge without the reality."[141]

It is no wonder that when they do occasionally come up with a solution to a social problem, it is an absurd *fatwa* that draws scorn from any man who has not abandoned reason. For example, a few years ago, the head of the Department of *Hadith* at al-Azhar University in

Cairo, the most prestigious university in Sunni Islam, issued a *fatwa* concerning the segregation of the sexes at work. He maintained that men and women can indeed work together, provided there is a "family bond" between them. To that end, he exhorted women to breastfeed their male colleagues *at least* five times to establish a familial relationship.[142] The *fatwa* was subsequently retracted and denounced by al-Azhar University, but the fact that a leading jurist at that institution could even come up with something like that reflects the deep intellectual malaise in the Muslim world.

The second sub-narrative is that in Islam there is one right way and one right answer to everything, right?

Quite the contrary. As far as non-fundamental religious principles are concerned, early Muslims were at ease with the existence of a spectrum of interpretations. As noted by Jonathan Brown, the Sunni Shariah tradition, "far from being a myopic or rigid body of law," was in fact a "swirl of stunning diversity," and "not only were there four distinct schools of law, but each school also had a range of opinions on any one question."[143] And even though scholars from different schools wrote "spirited polemics against one another, they still recognized each other's legitimacy" based on toleration of disagreement. In the 9th century, the Abbasid Caliphs even set up public debates on religion at the court.[144]

The move away from interpretational heterodoxy started to gain steam with the Ottomans, who were seeking to establish a unified set of laws to be applied across their empire. Thus, in the nineteenth-century, court judges who had previously enjoyed the freedom to issue rulings based on any school of law they saw fit in order to come up with the most equitable ruling, were restricted to just one.[145]

Matters grew worse at the end of the 18th century, as Muslims started to rapidly lose ground, not just in the realm of politics, but also in the realm of ideas. The rise and subsequent predominance of Western culture and Western values throughout the world caused many Muslims to withdraw culturally and intellectually into reactionary defensive positions that sought to hold these forces at bay.

This trend continues to this day, and Muslims show an overbearing commitment to orthodoxy and a deep suspicion, if not outright rejection, towards new ideas, especially ones that stray considerably from conventional wisdom. That is not to say that there is nothing to be garnered from the moral wisdom of ages past. As American scholar Richard M. Weaver wrote, when every man is "his own priest" and his "own professor of ethics," the result is anarchy.[146] Anyone who imagines otherwise is indulging in egotistical hubris. Civilization needs conservation. Indeed, immoderate criticism and a misguided breaking with the past are capable of doing an inordinate amount of harm.

However, taking all beliefs and practices handed down as axiomatic is also dangerous. Unfortunately, many Muslims today have unwittingly become the object of the Quranic warning about those who follow their forefathers blindly.

Islam has been impoverished by its own practitioners. It does not need to be reinvented but rather reconnected with its original dynamism, creativity, and confidence – traits that enabled Muslims in the past to adapt to new circumstances and challenges while also observing their faith.

The third sub-narrative is a pathological aversion to inquiry, particularly with regard to anything controversial.

Muslims in the Middle Ages studied, discussed, and dwelled on every minute aspect of Islamic theology in laborious detail. Back then, when people wrote critiques of Islam and scrutinized the religion and its founder, Muslims did not try to silence the detractors. They did not go to the streets and protest; neither did they go out for blood. Instead they wrote multi-volume intellectual rebuttals.

Today's Muslims, however, show nowhere near that level of intellectual rigor. If anything, they display a disturbing level of intellectual rigor mortis. They treat questions about Islam as the first step to disbelief.

Mind you, a Muslim has no problem utilizing his faculty for reason when talking about *other* religions. Debating an atheist, a Muslim will haughtily assert that atheism is absurd. After all, as the pre-Socratic philosopher Parmenides pointed out: something cannot come out of nothing. Should the atheist then ask, "Where does God come from then?" I assure you nine out of ten Muslims will be stumped and would seek God's refuge from Satan. It is blasphemy to ask such a question after all!

It is not. There are logical answers to the common atheist's riposte that even a child could understand. Most Muslims are unaware of them, because when Muslim children ask such questions, they are curtly told not to do so. From an early age, their spirit of natural inquisitiveness is suppressed in favor of rote memorization, regurgitation, and imitation.[a]

To make matters worse, religious education, both formal and informal, sweeps any controversial topic in Islamic history and Islamic theology under the proverbial rug.

This is done in good faith, to protect children and safeguard their faith from doubt. In the pre-internet age, it was inconsequential, in the same sense that a Native American living in pre-Columbian America was fine without vaccination. Not anymore.

This approach is responsible for creating an entire generation of Muslims who are intellectually defenseless in the face of even the most basic criticisms of Islam. A few YouTube videos are all it takes to rock some Muslims' faith to the very core.

Muslims need to approach religion differently. It should not be a thing handed down to us by people who have had it handed down to them. It should be a thing that is studied, discussed, reinterpreted, and adjusted to fit present circumstances. Excessive reverence that precludes

---

[a] In Arabic, the degree you get when you graduate is called an *ijaza* (permission)… that is permission to regurgitate what you have learned.

such an active approach kills faith. Because only such an approach can lead to genuine understanding. Without that, you cannot have conviction – you only have its counterfeit: credulity. That on its own cannot sustain faith, not in today's open marketplace of ideas, where there is no shortage of alternative narratives. Without the conviction that comes with genuine understanding, faith depreciates into ambivalence, then into irreligiousness, and then finally into disbelief.

This is the direction we are hurtling towards. If we maintain the present course, mosques in the Middle East will eventually be as empty as churches are nowadays in Europe.

Chapter 8

Love Thy Neighbors (Though They Will Burn in Hell)

A textbook for Grade 1 students in Palestine contains the following lovely picture.

The Arabic phrase on top is part of the last verse from the first chapter (*surah*) in the Quran, which is also recited during each of the five daily prayers which Muslims are commanded to perform.

> *In the name of Allah, the Entirely Merciful, the Especially Merciful*

> *[All] praise is due to Allah, Lord of the worlds -*

> *The Entirely Merciful, the Especially Merciful,*

> *Sovereign of the Day of Recompense,*

> *It is You we worship and You we ask for help.*

> *Guide us to the straight path -*

> *The path of those upon whom You have bestowed favor, **not of those who have evoked [Your] anger, or of those who are astray.***

Now, the Quran never specifies who are exactly those who have evoked his anger and those who are astray. However, it is classically interpreted in Islamic literature to refer to Jews and Christians respectively.

So in the picture, we see a little girl in a headscarf pointing presumably at a scene of Jews and Christian – including what appears to be women and children –

burning in hell. It is a scene of absolute human tragedy, and yet the girl is bright-eyed and has a wide Cheshire Cat smile on her face.[a]

Real people do not act this way. Even men who have been trained to kill do not behave like that. In a survey carried out by anthropologist David Marlowe after the first Gulf War, it was shown that witnessing harm to others, even to the enemy, is one of the most traumatic events that a soldier can experience.[147] How can an illustration of such utter inhumanity make its way into the national curriculum for first grade students in Palestine without anyone flagging it as inappropriate and obnoxious in the editorial process?

The answer is simple: because Muslims uphold the *dangerous narrative* that all non-Muslims are destined for hell.

The Quran does forewarn disbelievers with hellfire in a number of verses such as these: "And for those who disbelieve there will be the fire of hell..." (35:36) "And whoever desires other than Islam as religion, never will it be accepted from him, and he, in the Hereafter, will be among the losers." (3:85) But on the other hand, the Quran

---

[a] There is another way to interpret the illustration. The silhouetted people may actually represent Muslims on their way to heaven while the fire in the background engulfs everyone else. Either way, it's still a *dangerous narrative*.

also promises: "Those who believe, and those who are Jews, Christians, and Sabians – whoever believes in God and the Last Day, and does good deeds, will have their reward, and no fear will there be concerning them, nor will they grieve." (2:62) Yet in the Muslim world, far greater weight is attached to the verses that promise hell and eternal torment.

Thomas Hobbes noted, "While anyone is bound by his promise of something good, no one is bound by his threats; still less do threats bind God, who is infinitely more merciful than men."[148]

This distinction is lost on many Muslims.[a][149] Their preoccupation with the references to hell twists their view of the divine. It makes them see God in Old Testament terms, as a wrathful and jealous deity who will cast all the unbelievers into Gehenna.

In doing so, I believe Muslims do a great injustice to their creator. But their error is not merely a theological concern. It has social repercussions. Muslims are

---

[a] Evidence for this distinction can actually be found within the Quran itself. As remarked upon by Sayyid Qutb in his commentary on the Quran: "Every time the Qur'an states a definite promise or constant law, it follows it with a statement implying that the Divine will is free of all limitations and restrictions, even those based on a promise from Allah or a law of His. For His will is absolute beyond any promise of law."

commanded to show compassion and mercy to humankind, and they do show genuine compassion towards their non-Muslim neighbors and friends. Christians in particular are held in high esteem. Muhammad himself allowed Christians to perform their prayers in his mosque in Medina. [150] More recently, when Christian Tutsis and Christian Hutus were busy murdering each other during the Rwandan Genocide (with the explicit blessing of their priests), Muslims were among the few Rwandans who protected and hid both neighbors and strangers. [151]

As for Jews, despite the rampant use of antisemitic language in the Muslim world, Jews are also accepted as *ahl al-kitab* (People of the Book).[a] Muslims do not see Islam as a separate religion in as much as a culmination of previous creeds, mainly Judaism and Christianity.

Voltaire, speaking of French Catholics, once said, "We have enough religion to hate and persecute, but not enough to love and support."[152] Muslims, however, do not have that issue because they inexplicably hold within themselves both propositions. Despite being conscious of

---

[a] Strictly speaking, this phrase from the Quran applies only to faiths that possess a monotheistic scripture. Historically, however, early Muslims repurposed it, for political and humanistic reasons, so that even the Zoroastrian dualists of Persia and the polytheist pagans of India could be assigned this protected and privileged status.

the contradiction of said propositions, they reject neither. So Muslims who show great humanity in their dealing with "others" simultaneously maintain that "others" will eventually be cast into hell where they will burn for all eternity.

The danger of that narrative stems from the following issue: one cannot truly love humanity in general if they also hold true that most individual manifestations of it are destined to be *shish kebab* for eternity in the afterlife. If you maintain that another person is going to hell on the basis of their religion, your empathy for them diminishes because you are forced to conclude on some level that they must be evil or depraved. Otherwise, why would God, who is all-merciful and all-just, condemn them to eternal damnation? As Rousseau pointed out, to love people you regard as damned would be to hate God who punishes them.[153]

But what have non-believers done to be regarded as damned?

Well, they have denied Islam.

Islam is commonly regarded by Muslims as self-evident. Islam is called *din al-fitra* – the religion that is natural to man. Hence, it is inconceivable that a person does not recognize the truth to begin with. From Muslims' point of view, one look at the Quran with an open mind and you will convert on the spot. Other religions and lines of thought, however, are dismissed and belittled as irrational, *de haut en bas*.

A Muslim is quick to mock the irrationality of the Christian doctrine of the Trinity: "Three Gods in one, how does that make sense? How do the three Gods agree? What happened when God was human, did he go to the toilet?"

What Muslims do not realize is that Islam itself also has its fair share of narratives that require some degree of suspension of disbelief. God sends birds to bombard an army, which intended to raise the Kaaba to the ground, with baked clay. Muhammad mounts a Pegasus (or a winged centaur) and flies from Mecca to Jerusalem and then up to heaven in one night. He also splits the moon in two. A non-Muslim would find these accounts dubious, just as we do certain aspects of other faiths.

There are also topics in Islam and Islamic history that I struggled with for years. Only after a considerable amount of time, research, and personal experience was I able to reach an understanding or interpretation that I found satisfactory.

I find the idea that everything in Islam is instantly self-evident only rings true for one type of people: those who have been born into its lap and who have never bothered to look up criticisms of it. Unfortunately, such people constitute the overwhelming majority. Predicated on the assumption that any rational person would convert to Islam with even a minimal exposure to it, they get to the following conclusion: unbelievers – just like Satan – recognize Islam as true and then knowingly reject it out of arrogance or wickedness. Thus their non-belief in Islam is a matter of choice, an act of willful disobedience and depravity.

That is why no red flags where raised by the editors of the Palestinian textbook. The irony is that they might not actually hate Christians or Jews, but the *dangerous narrative* they uphold in the backs of their minds diminished their empathy and blinded them from seeing the depravity of that illustration.

In the words of Tariq Ramadan, Professor of Contemporary Islamic Studies at Oxford University, Muslims "have so much in common with Judaism and Christianity" and "with the values advocated by countless humanists, atheists, and agnostics."[154] When Muslims realize that, when they realize that their community is not comprised of those who are labeled as Muslim, but those that share their values and do good, they will not commit the sort of faux pas presented at the beginning of this chapter.

Chapter 9

Life, Liberty, and the Pursuit of Heretics

In February 2006, protests erupted around the world in Muslim cities. Three embassies were burned. Dozens were killed.

The reason? Cartoons.

On January 7, 2015, two brothers, armed with Kalashnikov rifles, stormed the offices of *Charlie Hebdo*, a French satirical weekly newspaper. They killed twelve people and injured eleven others.

The reason? Cartoons.

The cartoons in question were illustrations of the Prophet Muhammad that depicted him in a hideous manner. Naturally, as a Muslim, I find them repugnant. However, did these cartoons make me go berserk?

No.

Because I know better. I have studied Muhammad's life. The way he carried himself as a father, husband, leader, diplomat, and judge is inspirational. He was a noble man who showed compassion and mercy, even to his enemies. I know the cartoons are ahistorical. They could not be less accurate depictions of the real Muhammad, and so they neither detract from nor discredit him. On top of that, the cartoons themselves have no artistic, comedic, or intellectual merit and were designed purely for shock value. They were obviously bait – a cheap attempt to drive up the sales of an insignificant newspaper with minor circulation. Simply ignoring the cartoons would have condemned them to obscurity – exactly where they belong.

The larger Muslim community, however, immortalized the very images it so much abhorred. George Bernard Shaw once warned: "Don't wrestle with pigs. You both get dirty and the pig likes it." But being the reactionaries that they are, Muslims waded straight into the pig pen. By breaking out in violent protests, they turned the offensive cartoons into an emblem of free speech. And where there had only been one deplorable depiction of Muhammad, there emerged dozens, even hundreds.

Why did Muslims act like such complete dunces?

A part of it stems from Muslims' insecurity. The cartoons of Muhammad were not an attack on Muhammad in as much as they were an attack on the very identity of Muslims around the world, Muslims who are already suffering from a deep-seated inferiority complex. That is why it was just all too much for their porcelain-fragile egos. It is not that the Prophet was represented in a repulsive manner. If that were indeed the reason behind their outrage then Muslims would have been equally indignant by blasphemous portrayals of Jesus – not to mention God. As noted by Turkish writer Mustafa Akyol, the curious zealotry in the defense of Muhammad draws "from the fact that he is revered only by Muslims."[155] Hence when he is mocked, Muslims take it as a personal offense. We can see a similar pattern at a bar. When a bar patron becomes enraged because some bloke insulted his lady friend, the ensuing fistfight has nothing to do with the fair maiden and her slighted honor. The man turns to violence and risks jail time simply to maintain his own image. The cartoon protests are in the same vein.

Besides, if the plebs who took to the streets were primarily concerned with defending the Prophet, they would be angry at all the injustices within the Muslim world that make a mockery of his legacy. Where is the social justice that Muhammad advocated?

Muhammad emancipated many people. Muslim countries treat their foreign workers like slaves.

Muhammad treated his archenemies with mercy. Muslim countries torture and abuse their own citizens.

Muhammad consulted with his companions and led as first-among-equals rather than a king. Muslim countries are ruled with an iron fist by by potentates who care little for their subjects.

Muhammad treated his neighbors with compassion and required Muslims to do the same. Muslim countries squander their wealth on their inbred "princes" while people in neighboring countries starve to death.

And the list goes on…

If anyone has maligned the image of Muhammad, it is not the French newspaper *Charlie Hebdo* or the Danish newspaper *Jyllands-Posten* – it is Muslims themselves.

So the protests are mainly about Muslims' self-image, but there is one more factor, a *dangerous narrative*, that is in play here. It is the notion that ideas should be enforced, rather than be made to stand on their own by their own merit.

In 2013, an Egyptian university student and blogger professed his atheism and wrote some statements online that did not mesh with traditional Islamic narratives. So what happened? Did Egypt's al-Azhar University assign a couple of bright doctoral students from the department of theology to write a snappy rebuttal to the claims made by the blogger?

No. It was Egypt, so that was not how it panned out. Instead, three armored state security cars supported by an army vehicle raided his home in the middle of the night. They confiscated all his belongings, helped themselves to the money in his wallet, and threw him in jail.[156]

And for good measure, the university he was studying at failed him in every single course even though he had previously been at the top of his class.

This might be an extreme case, but in the Muslim world, reactions to ideas that run counter to orthodox beliefs are usually met with extreme hostility. The idea of engaging ideas at an intellectual level is a foreign one in this part of the world.

That is freedom of speech over here. It exists, as long as it is in line with Islam – or, more accurately, traditional interpretations thereof. It is no wonder that an increasing number of people in the West are coming to the conclusion that Islam is not compatible with the sacrosanct liberal value of freedom of speech.

After all, Muslim attitudes are a manifestation of Islamic values, aren't they? Not really. As noted in the Journal of Mass Communication and Journalism:

> Within the Quran, there is no text that forbids the freedom of expression, limits it to certain extents, or suppresses it by any means. On the contrary, the Quran encourages people to discuss matters openly, protest, accept ideas or reject them, and bring about all pretexts and evidences that might be available to contest Islamic teachings. The Quran puts no restrictions on the freedom of expression whatsoever.[157]

In fact, even Satan is allowed to speak openly! In the Quran (15:32–43), we are told of Satan's disobedience and the conversation that went on between him and God afterwards. In the conversation, Satan openly states that till the Day of

Judgement, he will deceive and mislead people, and yet he was not prevented from doing so. Satan's freedom of speech was not curtailed in any away, despite his ill intentions.

Isn't that proof of the sanctity of freedom of speech in Islam? If Satan, evil incarnate, is given the freedom to speak, by what right do Muslims use their religion to silence people with whom they disagree?[a]

Far from suppressing people, the Quran instructs Muslims to engage with nonbelievers in an open discussion, because it is understood that truth is reached through a process of dialectic. Hence, every side should be able to present their proofs and make their case without any kind of fear or intimidation.

Even if we were to disregard the scriptural angle concerning this issue, we would see that freedom of speech is good for Muslims, now more than ever.

---

[a] An important distinction: I am not making the case that freedom of speech should be absolute in every context. I am only making the case for it at an individual level within an interpersonal or literary medium. When media conglomerates broadcast the values of their corporate overseers to the masses and subvert established cultural norms under the banner "freedom of speech," I don't believe that should enjoy the same protections as an individual should have for speaking his mind. I think it's absurd that we allow the head of Disney, for example, to reach billions of children and inculcate them with whatever values he sees fit, with zero restriction, oversight, or accountability.

As noted by Mustafa Akyol in his article in the *New York Times*, the defense of Muslims who are threatened by the rise of Islamophobic forces lies within the protections offered by liberalism itself.[158] Muslims are able to practice their religion, dress freely in religious garb, build mosques, convert others to their faith, and preach their religion because of these protections.

One cannot support liberal values when it suits him and reject them when it does not. The accolades that Islam affords itself are in and of themselves in direct contravention of the beliefs of so many others. So at the end of the day, one can have either a liberal system or an illiberal one. Which is better?

I would say as long as Abdullah can practice his faith freely and be protected from discrimination, coming across an offensive cartoon is a small price for him to pay.

Having said that, it is also important to recognize that Muslims do in fact have reason to worry about the surge in anti-Muslim polemics. One cartoon or two, no matter how offensive, does not make much of a difference in the grand scheme of things. The European editor who publishes some nasty sketch thinking he is standing up for freedom of speech does not cause that much harm.

However, a pattern of misrepresentation across various media outlets and over a long period can indeed have dangerous consequences.

Take the Holocaust for example. That did not just happen in a cultural vacuum. German society had already been percolating with antisemitic rhetoric over several decades when it happened. From the 19th century, Jews were being represented as parasites on the Aryan nation. The systematic eradication of Jews would not have even been contemplated had the humanity of that minority group not been denied in the first place.

The Holocaust, of course, is not unique in that regard. Almost every act of genocide has been preceded by literature that seeks to demonize and dehumanize the eventual victims.

No government official in the Western world is calling for the internment of Muslims in concentration camps. I do not see myself reading a headline to that effect in tomorrow's newspaper. Nevertheless, as noted by sociologist Albert Bergesen, witch-hunts tend to happen in "dramatic outbursts."[159] The victims of the Reign of Terror and the Stalinist Show Trials were not lethargic or heedless. They were blindsided by the speed at which the mob went into a frenzy. Once a community is mobilized to purge itself from those it perceives as "internal enemies," things escalate quickly.

The consistent negative representation of Muslims is like deadwood piling up in the forest. Any spark can set the place ablaze.

On a small scale, this can lead to tragedies like the one that happened in Christchurch, where a gunman went on a shooting spree in two mosques in New Zealand, killing fifty-one people.[160] On a larger scale, however, and under certain social and political climates, the loss of empathy of a majority group towards a minority group can lead to genocide.

In his book *The End of Faith*, Sam Harris argues in favor of just such a scenario. He presents a hypothetical case in which an Islamist regime which "grows dewy-eyed at the mere mention of paradise" acquires nuclear weapons. Should that ever happen, Harris advocates a pre-emptive nuclear strike on the Muslim world. "Tens of millions of innocent civilians" would be killed, he concedes; however, he assures his readers that such an "unthinkable crime" would be "the only course of action available."[161]

To begin with, this whole scenario is based on the premise that intelligence about the possession of weapons of mass destruction is reliable. However, as the Second Persian Gulf War has demonstrated, that is not case. The United States invaded Iraq on the pretext that it possessed weapons of mass destruction, and yet despite all efforts, the U.S.-led coalition could not find any evidence to support that claim. So it is hard to ascertain if a country has really acquired weapons of mass destruction. Hence any pre-emptive nuclear strike against "tens of millions of innocent civilians" would not be based on clear cut evidence but on mere suspicion. The case suffers from the same flaw present in the "ticking bomb" problem, which questions the morality of torturing someone if they have knowledge of a live bomb somewhere in the city. Such cases look clean because on paper there is no room for ambiguity. In reality, however, things are not so simple, because in real life one cannot tell with absolute certainty if the captured "terrorist" is actually a terrorist or some unfortunate chap that intelligence services have mistaken for one.

But I digress.

Imagine if Harris had made a similar case against a state which unquestionably possesses nuclear weapons, say a state like Israel – a state which, according to Israeli Professor Avi Shlaim of Oxford University, fulfills all the criteria of a "rogue state" and is ruled by "an utterly unscrupulous set of leaders."[162] A state which incidentally also grows dewy-eyed over the notion of establishing *Eretz Yisrael* and espouses deeply troubling millenarian as well as supremacist narratives. As noted by Israeli historian Yuval Noah Harari, Jewish orthodoxy holds that "Jews are intrinsically superior to all other humans" and that "the life of a Jew is more valuable than the life of a Gentile."[163a] Israel-based journalist and filmmaker David Sheen provides countless examples of such *dangerous narratives* from mainstream religious and political figures in Israel, which include calls for expansionist war, genocide, and bringing back slavery, among other things.[164]

Imagine then if Harris had argued that for the sake of world peace it would be fine to kill nine million Israelis on account of the nuclear capabilities of their belligerent government and the disturbing narratives that run deep in their society.

---

[a] According to the Babylonian Talmud, for example, a Jew is allowed to desecrate the Sabbath to save the life of another Jew, but is forbidden to do so if a Gentile's life is in danger.

Would Harris be published if he were to champion such views? Would he be considered a mainstream intellectual and invited to give a talk at the Oxford Union? No, he would have been branded *persona non grata* – and with good reason, I might add – for defending genocide.

But suggesting the killing of "tens of millions of innocent civilians" apparently does not fall outside the Overton window, because as long as one is discussing Muslims, "unthinkable crimes" are not so unthinkable after all.

And keep in mind, Sam Harris is not the only, or even the worst, offender. Here is some of the rhetoric being peddled on Islam and Muslims. Keep in mind, these statements were not pulled from The Daily Stormer or far-right blogs. These are statements made by mainstream figures and media outlets.

> "Muslims are a threat to our way of life."[165] (The Telegraph)

> "It is the black heart of Islam, not its black face, to which millions object."[166] (The Telegraph)

> "... where there are mosques, there are Muslims, and where there are Muslims, there are problems."[167] (New York Post)

"They're the ones who are perverted. They are the ones who are dangerous. They are the ones who are subhuman. They are the ones who are human debris…"[168] (Rush Limbaugh)

"We should invade their countries, kill their leaders and convert them to Christianity."[169] (Ann Coulter)

"These people need to be forcibly converted to Christianity… It's the only thing that can probably turn them into human beings."[170] (Michael Savage)

"Islam is the greatest force for evil in the world today. I've said so, often and loudly."[171] (Professor Richard Dawkins)

"Islam is the problem."[172] (Boris Johnson)

"Conditions for Muslims in Europe must be made harder across the board."[173] (Douglas Murray)

"We need a final solution."[174] (Katie Hopkins)

When radio presenters are calling for a "final solution," should Muslims be wary? Should they seek better representation in the media? Most certainly, they should. But not through violence or protests.

As Mustafa Akyol eloquently put it, "The power of any faith … comes not from its coercion on critics and dissenters but from the moral integrity and the intellectual strength of its believers."[175] Hence anti-Muslim polemics should be handled intellectually and with dignity. This is a battle that should be fought with books, papers, seminars, and lectures by scholars and public intellectuals… not by the *hoi polloi*. And it should be clear from the start that the goal is not to award Muslims or Islam a special status, but to prevent the worst atrocities of the 20th century from happening all over again.

Chapter 10

Muslim Angry Birds: A History of Histrionics

Picture a crowd of Muslims. What image comes to mind?

Did you picture a crowd of Muslims at a concert? Did you picture them at a marathon or a fundraiser?

You probably did not. You did not even picture a crowd. You pictured a mob, a mob made up of churlish boors holding placards and thrusting their fists in the air. You pictured their faces contorted in anger, each framing a gaping mouth. A grubby, unwashed, bellicose multitude with the capacity to antagonize from a hundred yards.

That image does not come to mind because of some deep-seated racism towards Muslims. It comes to mind because it happens so often. When *Newsweek* did a cover story about it entitled "Muslim Rage," it was met unsurprisingly with angry protests and Muslim rage.[176]

In physics, Newton's third law states, "Every action produces an equal and opposite reaction." Muslims, however, have their own law: for every action there is a greater and disproportionate reaction.

But why act in that manner? Could they be following in the footsteps of the Prophet?

No. If we look at Muhammad's life we see that he never acted with anger and wanton violence, even though he was subjected to every manner of insult and abuse. He was spat on, rubbish and animal intestines were dumped on him, stones were hurled at him, food was denied him, assassins were sent after him, and he was exiled from his home. Yet he endured all of that with so much dignity and grace that many of his former enemies accepted his message and became his staunchest allies.

And as if the example he set could not have made it any clearer, Muhammad counseled Muslims again and again: "Don't get angry."

So what explains Muslims' anger management problems? To understand, we need to take a look at another *dangerous narrative.*

In the West, emotional incontinence is viewed as a sign of weakness. A person who displays extreme emotions is someone who has lost control. That is why, in the West, people will go to extreme lengths to hide their emotions.

In the Muslim world, nowadays, conspicuous outbursts of emotions in full public view do not suffer from such a stigma. On the contrary, they are sometimes seen as a bona fide sign of one's authenticity, if not righteousness. It is the Cartesian School of moral epistemology: I am angry, therefore I am right. The angrier a person, the more right he must be. After all, the profundity of a person's response is proportional to the volume and shrillness of his outrage or lamentation.

For that reason, incendiary outrage, which can often be literally incendiary, has been the go-to weapon of choice in Muslims' moral arsenal. From an invasion of a Muslim country to a Muhammad cartoon, whenever there is a situation that draws Muslims' ire, we are presented with a *tableau vivant* of angry Muslims screaming and snarling, more orc than human.

This has several effects, all of them negative.

First, expressions of extreme anger are difficult to relate to. Who watched *The Lord of the Rings* and sympathized with the feral orcs? No one. The West might have a fascination with the concept of the "noble savage," but no one has a thing for actual savages or those who present themselves in that light. As a rule of thumb, whoever looks the angriest loses.

If Muslims want to be seen as nice and reasonable, they have to look nice and reasonable. Proverbs about books and covers aside, fact is, people do judge books by their covers. Muslims should be conscious of the image they are conveying so that they are seen how they want to be seen.

Second, as pointed out by Theodore Dalrymple, the public display of extreme emotions suffers from an "inflationary pressure." After all, there is no point in displaying those emotions in a way no one notices. For that reason, "more and more extravagant [and extreme] displays of emotions become necessary," not because they are warranted but merely to "compete with others and be remarked upon." [177] The so-called "Arab Spring" demonstrations, for example, were not set in motion until someone literally set himself on fire in front of a police station in Tunisia. Had the emotional currency in this part of the world not been so debased by the routine and excessive display of emotions, it would have taken far less to galvanize people.

Third, also as pointed out by Dalrymple:

When sentimentality becomes a mass public phenomenon… it becomes manipulative in an aggressive way: it demands of everyone that he join in. A man who refuses to do so, on the grounds that he does not believe that the purported object of sentiment is worthy of demonstrative display, puts himself outside the pale of the virtuous and becomes almost an enemy of the people. His fault is a political one, a refusal to recognize the truth of the old saw, *vox populi, vox dei* – the voice of the people is the voice of God. Sentimentality then becomes coercive.[178]

As a person who lives in a Muslim country and harbors unorthodox views that clash with those held by mainstream society, this passage resonates with me on a fundamental level. The stakes of standing up for the truth in the Muslim world are indeed high. Around here, certain views, if publicly expressed, will not only turn you into a social pariah, but can literally land you in jail or even cost you your life.

Fourth, instead of tackling problems in a determined and rational manner, extreme emotionalism "enables the government to throw sops to the public."[179] This is why political discourse in the Muslim world amounts to nothing more than bombastic rhetoric and emotional drivel that seeks to tug on heartstrings and prod emotional soft spots. Politicians, demagogues, and potentates in this part of the world are not leaders, they are dealers of emotional sedatives to sentimental junkies.

Fifth, extreme emotions cause Muslims to lose sight of everything else. Under their effect, complex thoughts and subtlety get overridden by one need – expression. In a state of maudlin public sentimentality, as Dalrymple puts it, "the person is more moved by the fact that he is moved than moved by whatever is supposedly moving him, and furthermore is concerned that everyone should see just how moved he is."[180] In other words, the emotions themselves and the expression of said emotions become ends in themselves. While this might have its place in modern art, in real life expression untutored by thought and sans purpose, is unproductive at best, counterproductive at worst.

When Omar the teenage Palestinian throws rocks at Israeli soldiers, he expresses his anger. He might indeed be justified, and it might even be emotionally gratifying for young Omar. The question that should be asked, however, is: does it alleviate his situation or exacerbate it?

Unfortunately, a large percentage of Muslims do not think so far. In that sense, they are like Pavlovian dogs. Whenever triggered, they can be counted on to produce the same brainless, reactionary response. They are fixated on the expression of their umbrage and are blind to the consequences of that expression.

Seen through that lens, you start to understand why the Israeli-Palestinian conflict, or any conundrum in which Muslims are involved, is so difficult to resolve. When you are unable to deal with a problem in a rational and unemotional manner, you cannot see it to a satisfactory conclusion.

Sixth, Muslim emotionalism lends itself to an episodic and reactionary frame of mind – a peek-a-boo world, where now this event, now that, occupies their full attention, before then being promptly forgotten.

Emotions flare up quickly but cool down just as fast. If a person's actions are predicated on his emotions, what you get is a great flurry of action, followed by a long period of passivity. This is the pattern you see played out in protests. What is on display in most demonstrations is just the byproduct of an intense emotional reaction. Once the emotions simmer down, all the wind is sucked out of the demonstration and things settle down. That is until another issue comes up that causes Muslims to get triggered. Then the cycle repeats itself.

It is the Muslim version of *Groundhog Day*.

However, whereas the film had a happy ending, the real life Muslim version does not lend itself to one, because extemporaneous flurries of action are destructive by nature. They do not lead to sustainable positive change. It works if you want to overthrow a regime or create mayhem. But if your goal is constructive, it does not help.

Positive change requires a long-term proactive mindset and a consistent pattern of behavior. Issues should not be looked at in terms of how they make a person feel but in terms of the steps that are needed to rectify them.

Blaise Pascal once said: *"Travaillons donc à bien penser"* (Let us labor, therefore, to think well). That is good advice that Muslims would be wise to heed. For until they labor to do so, they will just remain angry and impotent. They will continue to work themselves into indiscriminate fits of rage at every injustice *de jour*, and in the end all the strutting and fretting, all the sound and fury, will amount to nothing.

Chapter 11

Islam: Religion or Shibboleth?

Over the past year, scandals revolving around the sexual impropriety of renowned Muslim preachers have rocked Muslim communities. People split into two camps. Some rushed to defend their beleaguered preachers, whom they follow on social media platforms. While others condemned them as hypocrites, people who do not practice what they preach.

Even if some of the allegations are false, there is enough evidence to indicate that some are true. So people's reaction in the first camp can be dismissed as denial. But what about the verdict cast by people in the second camp? Are the preachers really hypocrites because they were exposed of having feet of clay?

I think it is an oversimplification to think of them as such. These people might actually believe in what they preach despite indulging or having indulged at some point in their life in a vice opposite a virtue they call for. The incongruity between their preaching and their conduct has its roots in something deeper than mere hypocrisy or moral infirmity. It has its roots in a *dangerous narrative*.

All the accused preachers have one thing in common: none of them are converts. They were all born into the religion. None of them had to undergo any behavioral changes to become Muslim. They were all labeled Muslim from the get go. For them, religious identity is not acquired but assigned. It has less to do with beliefs and piety and more to do with the social and cultural milieu in which they were raised. It is like being Catholic in Ireland.

To demonstrate that, ask Muslims born into the religion to list the five pillars of Islam from the top of their heads. Many who count themselves as Muslim would actually struggle with that question.

And speaking of the five pillars of Islam, there are many Muslims who fast but do not pray. But aside from those who abstain from fasting for medical reasons, you would be hard-pressed to find any Muslim who prays but does not fast. Why is this so when both acts are among the five pillars of Islam?

Because there is a strong cultural element to fasting. Muslims will assert that they fast for God, but if that were the only reason an equal number would pray as well. I would argue that many people fast because it is a shared experience. They fast because it strengthens their ties with their social circle. It gives them a sense of belonging. In that equation, God is an afterthought.

So what happens when Islam becomes a cultural identity? What happens when Muslims attach too much weight to *being* a Muslim rather than *behaving* like one?

It fosters a tribal mentality, one that revolves around "in-group loyalty and out-group hostility, even when members of one's own group are acting in abhorrent ways."[181] We saw this in Rotherham, England. In that working town of 260,000 residents, organized gangs comprised mainly of Pakistani men sexually abused and pimped more than 1400 white British girls – some as young as eleven years old. This took place over the course of several years. [182] Some people in that community, beginning with the friends and family of the perpetrators, must have had an inkling of what was going on. Yet they all turned a blind eye, and none of them reported a crime.

We also witness this tribal mentality in the timid reaction of Muslims to Saudi atrocities in Yemen. Between April 2015 and October 2018, *eighty-five thousand* children under the age of five died of starvation in Yemen and *fourteen million* people there are "on the brink of starvation."[183] It is being called "the worst humanitarian crisis in the world." Yet Muslims have remained despicably quiet. So it comes as no surprise that when Saudi Arabia bombed a school bus with 40 children on board[184], there were no calls in the Muslim world for sanctions on that country or a boycott of its products. What are forty dead school children blown to pieces compared to eighty-five thousand starved to death? When Saudi Arabia dispatched a hit squad to assassinate Jamal Khashoggi, a US-based journalist and critic of Saudi Arabia's government, in its own consulate in Istanbul and cut him to pieces with a bone saw,[185] people in the Middle East did not deplore his murder. Instead they made lighthearted jokes about it and shared them on social media.

Imagine, however, the reaction if Khashoggi had been assassinated with the same brutality at an Israeli consulate. Imagine the outpouring of moral outrage if Israel were responsible for killing eighty-five thousand Palestinian children. But for Yemen, nary a peep, much less a roar, ensues from the Muslim world, because the vile murderers are Muslim.

At an individual level, people who are born into Islam and who have their identity conferred at birth grow to see themselves as virtuous without having to do anything. This unearned sense of moral superiority diminishes the importance of achievement and conduct in defining one's identity. One is not motivated to act in a righteous manner if they are labeled as righteous or superior to begin with. So instead of being righteous, they become self-righteous, perpetually immersed in a tepid bath of self-esteem and self-congratulation.

This pattern is not exclusive to Islam. It is problematic in any belief system that binds one's salvation primarily to the acceptance of a few abstract concepts. A lot of devout Christians, for example, treat the Ten Commandments as the Ten Optional Suggestions. They are not hypocrites, it is just that they believe they have already been saved. As pointed out by Nietzsche, the central axiom in Protestant Christianity, that the burden of redemption was borne by Christ during his crucifixion, removes moral responsibility from his followers because, in a sense, Jesus has done all the moral heavy lifting.[186] Paul confirms that in his epistle when he writes that man is glorified solely by faith, not by work.[187] Taking this principle to its logical conclusion, one sees that it is redundant, for salvation's sake, to imitate Christ and manifest his values in one's behavior and words. A few effortless thoughts, after all, and you are guaranteed salvation and eternal bliss. Under these conditions, religion ceases to be a system of moral conduct and becomes a label. When that happens, transgressions follow.

This mindset is even more pernicious in the Muslim world. Over here, moral behavior is not internally driven, it is externally compelled. It is shame based, not guilt based. Many people in the Muslim world live in an upstanding manner not because they are morally upright but because of the social stigma that would befall them if they did not heed social conventions. Muslims live in a perpetual fear of the wagging tongues of their neighbors. "What will the neighbors say?" is one of their top concerns. Morality is not the realm of the individual, it is the realm of the collective – the group.

And within a communal framework, that system can be quite effective. It works as long as one lives in a tightly knit group where he would never dare incur the opprobrium of his family and community. However, the system breaks down without that deterrent. In today's world, where Muslims are increasingly pursuing atomized lives outside the circle they were born into, that is often the case. This explains why many Muslims, especially ones from conservative communities, who lived more-or-less pious lives in their home country, spiral out of control when they move to the West. With the absence of collective pressure, they are no longer compelled to be the "good girl" or the "good boy." They are free to indulge in all the temptations that were hitherto too socially costly under the Argus-eyed scrutiny of their family and community. And indulge they do, because for those who have not developed an internal moral compass, freedom devolves into license. And with license, the Dionysian overpowers the Apollonian. Sex, drugs, alcohol… anything goes. One thing they do retain, though, is their "Muslim" identity which serves as a cushion to lean on in times of spiritual crisis.

This schizophrenic disconnect between beliefs and behavior in the Muslim world will not be bridged until Muslims stop associating virtue with the label of Islam and realize that, as Aleksandr Solzhenitsyn observed, "the line dividing good and evil cuts through the heart of every human being."[188] Virtue is not a byproduct of an assumed identity or religious beliefs, since religious belief is merely a compass for virtue, not a manifestation of virtue per se. Virtue is achieved through actions. It is the measure of living in line with the values of Islam, which in secular terms are to a large extent embodied in old fashioned bourgeois values – prudence, thrift, industry, honesty, moderation, politeness, and restraint. For that reason virtue is never final. It is something that requires eternal vigilance, because it depends on the choices we make every single day.

Thomas Hobbes once wrote that God promised heaven to those "who walk through this world according to the commands and limits prescribed by Him."[189] No one can demand a right to Paradise on the grounds of a label. We can merit paradise only through what we do, not what we choose to call ourselves. God looks at persons not personas. Muslims would be wise to keep that in mind.

Chapter 12

Pride and Prejudice and Muslims

More than thirteen centuries before Martin Luther King gave his famous speech "I Have a Dream," Muhammad told Muslims in his last sermon:

> All mankind is from Adam and Eve, an Arab has no superiority over a non-Arab, nor a non-Arab has any superiority over an Arab; also a white has no superiority over a black, nor a black has any superiority over a white - except by piety and good action.[190]

In Islam, unlike Christianity, the Hamitic curse does not exist. There is no scriptural support for any notion of racial superiority. On the contrary, the religion itself is racially egalitarian.

Historically, the Muslim world reflected this progressive view. From the Abbasid Caliphate in the 9th century to the Ottoman Empire in the 19th, Muslim states where marked by their diversity.[191]

However, with the breakup of the Ottoman Empire at the beginning of the 20th century, racial and religious diversity were lost. The newly formed states were largely mono-ethnic and mono-religious.

The political class of these states made use of that to rationalize their usurpation of power and legitimize their rule. Politicians like Mustafa Kemal Ataturk in Turkey and Gamal Abdel Nasser in Egypt pushed an ethno-nationalist worldview. Shared heritage was not only ignored but actively effaced. No measure to turn that worldview into accepted dogma was spared. In Turkey, for example, Ataturk Latinized the Turkish alphabet overnight by official decree. His reason for doing so was, by his own admission, "to cleanse the Turkish mind from its Arabic roots."[192]

Ataturk's successor and close friend İsmet İnönü reiterated that point in his memoir, *Hatıralar*:

The goal of the alphabet reform is not to raise the literacy rate… [but] to close the doors of the past to the newer generations, break the ties with the Arab-Muslim world, and to lessen the influence of religion on the public. Newer generations would not learn the old script and we would control the works written in the new script.[193]

In addition to the changes introduced to the Turkish alphabet, Turkey imposed an aggressive policy of Turkification on its minorities. The teaching of Arabic, for example, was banned and Kurds "were forced to pay a fine for each Kurdish word that they uttered."[194]

These measures succeeded – if one can indeed call retrogression a success – in Balkanizing the Muslim world. The race-blind camaraderie that marked race relations in earlier epochs was superseded by sentiments of contempt and denigration towards those outside the newly defined in-group.

To this day, Muslims societies are plagued by this. Even in the presence of educated and refined company, one can hear statements that would make a politically correct westerner go into epileptic shock. Entire races are nonchalantly described as dirty, niggardly, ragged, or unrefined.

In fact, often no adjective is used at all. The words "Arab," "Kurd," or "Indian" have themselves become pejoratives, as these words have been repurposed from connotatively neutral designations of race into racial slurs. For example, a Turk would call someone an "Arab," and an Arab would call someone a "Kurd," in the same sense that a racist in America would call a black person the N-word.

That mentality is not reserved for people of other races. It exists even within the same ethnic group. For example, Levantine Arabs look down on Gulf Arabs, while Gulf Arabs look down on Egyptian Arabs. Even when the focus is narrowed down to sub-ethnic groups, the problem persists. For example, Levantine Arabs from Lebanon look down on Levantine Arabs from Syria and Palestine, while Gulf Arab from Saudi Arabia and the United Arab Emirates look down on Gulf Arabs from Yemen.

This prejudice is sometimes carried *ad absurdum* to ever-increasing granularity. In one case I am familiar with, a man's choice of spouse was spurned by his parents. Their reason? While the girl in question was indeed from the same city, she hailed from a different neighborhood. That alone made her *persona non grata* and an object of scorn.

This kind of behavior is expressly forbidden in Islam. The Quran says:

> O you who have believed, let not a people ridicule [another] people; perhaps they may be better than them; nor let women ridicule [other] women; perhaps they may be better than them. And do not insult one another and do not call each other by [offensive] nicknames. Wretched is the name of disobedience after [one's faith]. And whoever does not repent   then it is those who are the wrongdoers. (49:11)

We see stories to the same effect in the *Hadith*. One time, when a man used a racial slur, Muhammad summoned him and admonished him thusly:

> You still retain the standards and judgments of the pre-Islamic days of ignorance. Islam has eradicated all these false standards or measures judging people by blood, fame, color, or wealth. It has established that the best and most honorable of men is he who is the most pious and upright in conduct.[195]

Yet despite Islam's position on this topic, Muslims refuse to let go of the *dangerous narrative* that proclaims ascendancy based on race and other superficialities. This is inimical to Muslims' interest because in so doing they blind themselves to opportunities for cooperation with people of different backgrounds – just when they are in most need of such opportunities.

Finally, there are two more *dangerous narratives* which lead to prejudice in the Muslim world and need to be addressed: guilt by group association and guilt by historical association.

To explain these two narratives, I will use antisemitism in the Muslim world as a frame of reference. The political situation in the Middle East has indeed tainted the relations between Muslims and Jews, but I posit that that animosity is maintained to a large extent by these two *dangerous narratives*.

Muslims do not discern that Jews are not a monolithic group. When they think of Jews, they think Netanyahu or AIPAC. But in reality neither is representative of all Jews. When President Trump issued his infamous "Muslim travel ban," liberal Jews in the United States were among the first to rush to the aid of

Muslims. Eighteen Jewish organizations called on Congress to lift Trump's executive order.[196] Such stories unfortunately often pass unnoticed by the Muslim community, and the realization that Muslims have many allies within the Jewish community is sadly overlooked.

Perhaps more dangerous than guilt by group association, is guilt by historical association. Muslims view Jews through the prism of political events that took place in the formative years of Islam. Modern Jews are equated with the Jews of Khaybar, who violated their treaty with Muhammad and conspired to murder him.

These two *dangerous narratives* are encapsulated in a phrase that Muslims often chant in political rallies denouncing Israel: "*Khaybar, Khabybar, ya Yahud; Jaishu Muhammad sa ya'ud*" (Kahybar, Khaybar, O Jews. The Army of Muhammad will return).[197]

Phonetically, it is quite catchy in Arabic. Its implications, though, are not as jovial. To charge modern day Jews with responsibility over what some of their ancestors did in the 7th century is to mark that entire community with an original sin – and the thing with original sins is that they are almost impossible to absolve oneself from. Christians had to send God on a suicide mission to get rid of theirs.

So by effect, when Muslims ascribe guilt to Jews by historical association, they preclude any chance for harmonious co-existence with that entire community, for there can be no peace with those who are deemed inherently wicked.

These narratives are not exclusively applied to Jews. We see these narratives in play, though to a lesser effect, in Muslims' view of any community that they had significant interaction with in the past. For example, Muslims' view of Western Christians is rooted in the Crusades. That is why the word for "Westerner" in Arabic is *frenji* (Frank) in reference to Frankish crusaders. Furthermore, polemics against the West often evoke the Crusades as if there is some direct link between the modern West and those who answered the call of Pope Urban II and marched on Jerusalem.

Ironically the counter to both these *dangerous narratives* can be found in the Quran: "And no bearer of burdens will bear the burden of another..." (35:18). Guilt by both group association and historical association are alien to Islam.

Unfortunately, we have too much religiosity yet too little religion in the Muslim world, so what Islam actually says on the matter is ignored, and the crowds continue to clamor: "*Kahybar, Khaybar, ya Yahud*" as if it is the will of God.

Chapter 13

Muslim Women: Les Misérables?

Fatma is a woman whose poor fortune saw her born in a Muslim country. She was never given a proper education. She is confined to her home most of the time. When she does go out, she is made to wear a stifling black beekeeper outfit that conceals her from head to toe. She is bossed around by the men in her family and was forced into an arranged marriage at the tender age of nine. One faux pas and she will have her throat slit by her male relatives in an "honor killing." And to top it all, her genitals were mutilated at birth.

Such a wretched thing, this Fatma. It is good, then, that for the most part, she is just the product of an orientalist fantasy.

In an earlier chapter, I discussed how Muslims are so fond of stereotypes. However, when it comes to the portrayal of women in Muslim societies, it is Westerners who have fallen into this habit. Fatma has more in common with the trope of the damsel in distress than with women in the Muslim world.

That is not to say that there aren't any women anywhere in the Muslim world who are oppressed and who do lead miserable lives.

In places like Afghanistan, and in other uneducated poverty-stricken rural communities, there are cases with a lot in common with the apocryphal Fatma.

Ayaan Hirsi Ali asserts that "women in Islam are oppressed"[198] and that "no group is more harmed by sharia than Muslim women."[199] In similar fashion, Sam Harris claims that "nobody suffers the consequences of Islam more than [Muslim women]"[200] and that in Islam "the central message is that women are second-class citizens and the property of the men in their lives."[201] Christian Evangelist Franklin Graham goes even further. "The brutal, dehumanizing treatment of women by the Taliban has been well documented", he states. "The abusive treatment of women in Muslim countries is nearly as draconian."[202]

Though spoken with vehemence and authority, it only takes one semester of a study-abroad program in a Muslim country for such statements, and perhaps the people behind them, to be stripped from any shred of credibility. The Western narrative that pictures Muslim women as wretched, submissive wallflowers is fallacious. Even back in seventh century Arabia, it was not so. As noted by Reza Aslan, women in Muhammad's time prayed and even fought alongside men.[203] Now, of course, I am not implying that the last part was a common occurrence. Most women would not have been physically up to the task. Besides, from an evolutionary perspective, they are too valuable to send to war. A society can survive the death of most of its men, but it cannot survive the death of most of its women. The point I am making here is that in cases where the women insisted on joining the army for personal reasons, they were allowed to do so. This shows there was neither a scriptural directive nor a societal precept that denied women the right to participate in public life.

Some women even managed to take leadership roles – religious, political, and, at least on one occasion, military.[204] The best example of this is Muhammad's young wife Aisha. Far from being a victimized girl as anti-Islamic polemics claim, Aisha was a senior bearer of

Islam's teaching. Much of what we know about Muhammad's life actually comes from her. That is in addition to being the head of a faction in Islam's first civil war (a role she admittedly later regretted).[205]

Another illustrious example from that time period showcasing how women sometimes played influential roles in the public sphere is Fatima al-Fihri. In 859 AD, Fatima founded and supervised the construction of the oldest surviving university in the world in Fez, Morocco.[206]

Lady Mary Wortley Montagu, an 18th century English aristocrat who lived for some time in Ottoman Istanbul, mocked those who lament the state of Muslim women:

> Tis also very pleasant to observe how tenderly he and all his brethren voyage-writers lament the miserable confinement of the Turkish ladies, who are perhaps more free than any ladies in the universe... Turkish ladies have, at least, as much wit and civility, nay liberty, as among us.[207]

Just to put that into perspective, French women living in the Land of Égalité did not attain full capacity before the law until 1938, a right that Islam granted women as early as the seventh century.[208]

What about today? The mass of Muslim women, to borrow a phrase from Henry David Thoreau, lead lives of quiet desperation. Don't they?

Not according to Dr. Margaret Nydell. Nydell, who has actually lived and worked across various countries in the Arab world, states in her book that the folk knowledge on Muslim women that depicts them as oppressed, servile, and without rights is usually based either on outdated information or on the worst possible examples. These examples are usually taken from Afghanistan, Saudi Arabia, and Iran – three countries which are the exception rather than the rule in the Muslim world. "Most Muslim women," she states, are in fact "happy in their lives"[209] and "feel satisfied that the present social system provides them with security, protection, and respect."[210]

But how is that possible? Isn't the Muslim world plagued with polygamy and child-marriage?

No, it is not. You would not know that from Ayaan Hirsi Ali, Sam Harris, or the legion of right-leaning YouTube commentators, but the fact is, these are not rampant issues in the Muslim world. Only about one to two percent of married men have more than one wife.[211] That is because even though Islam theoretically allows up to four wives, it is not an option except for the filthy rich who can afford it and the dirt poor whose lifestyle does not incur large expenses. Personally, even though I was raised in the Middle East, I have never met even one person with multiple wives.

As for child marriage, yes it does exists in destitute communities, but it is not driven by faith. It is driven by crushing financial need. The Yemeni and Somali parents who sell their daughters into a marriage are not driven by religious or oppressive patriarchal traditions. They are driven by economic factors – the same ones that drive Russian parents in Siberia to pimp their twelve-year-old daughters to "modeling" agencies.[212]

Even in oil-rich countries where you find women covered head to toe in a *burqa*, they generally have it really good. Most are so rich that they do not have to work a day their entire lives. They wake up whenever they want, travel wherever they want, and do whatever they please. They even have a retinue of servants at their beck and call.

I am not defending the *burqa* in any way. I think it is a daft cultural relic with no basis in religion.[a] But before you feel sorry for the ladies in drapes, keep in mind that those women often lead *Downton Abbey* fat-cat lifestyles. Many women in the West would gladly don a beekeeper outfit and give up their right to vote for good measure if they could live such pampered lives.

Having said that, does that mean there aren't any *dangerous narratives* affecting women in Muslim societies?

Indeed there are. For starters, conservative Muslims are obsessed with segregating men from women and limiting the interaction between the two. From weddings to ISNA conferences held in the United States, a great deal of effort has been spent separating the boys from the girls. In Saudi Arabia, even fast food restaurants have different spaces for men and women. If a couple is seen enjoying a Big Mac together, a member of the religious police can interrupt their meal and ask them to show proof that they are married. If they are not, they could be thrown in jail.

---

[a] The *burqa* which covers the entire body including the face is not to be confused with the *hijab* or headscarf which resembles a nun's habit. The *hijab*, unlike the *burqa*, does have scriptural basis in the *hadith*.

Yet in Mecca, Islam's holiest city, men and women have always prayed side by side as a single undivided community, and it has been like that since the time of Muhammad.

The fact that men and women can occupy the same space in Mecca but not in McDonald's shows that segregation of the sexes is not a heavenly mandate but a man-made rule. Actually, the practice of segregating spaces based on gender started several decades after the death of Muhammad. It was borrowed from Persian and Byzantine culture where it was customary for upper-class women to be secluded from all men outside their families.[213]

Then there is the issue of double standards in Muslim societies. Men are afforded many liberties. A young man can stay out late, go on dates, have a relationship, and sometimes even drink alcohol without as much as a raised eyebrow from his parents. If a woman wanted to live like that, however, she would be in for a stiff fight, unless she came from a very liberal family.

I am not saying here that women should also live like libertines, but I am saying that Muslims should be consistent about their values. If a certain behavior is wrong, it is wrong regardless what gonads the perpetrator happens to have. In America, in the 1600s, if a boy was seen conversing with a girl he was not related to, they did not chastise the girl and let the boy go scot free. Far from it. The boy in that case was publicly whipped.[214] Harsh though it may have been, at least they applied their values consistently.

With Muslims, though, observing and manifesting values is less important than the appearance of doing so. What matters is face. A boy cannot get pregnant, so whatever debauchery he partakes in cannot leave any visible mark. That is why a boy is never the victim of an "honor killing." A girl, however, is only a broken condom away from a big belly, and so her behavior is constantly scrutinized.

This narrative that holds women accountable for their conduct but turns a blind eye on how men carry themselves needs to end. Not only is it unfair to women, but it is also detrimental for men, for such an approach is not conducive to raising men of quality, men who will not shirk responsibility but bear the burden of being and the vicissitudes of life as gravely as they bear the responsibility of a relationship.

However, contrary to all the narratives explored thus far, the most ruinous *dangerous narrative* in the Muslim world is not something that originated from within but something we have rather foolishly imported: feminism.

Muslim women are not under threat from a particular article of dress or prudish social norms. What actually endangers their well-being are the feminist tropes they are adopting from progressives in the West without due diligence.

At the far end of the spectrum, there are those who have embraced the notion that marriage is a system of patriarchal oppression inimical to the interests of women. In line with Marx, Engels, and the utopian socialists, they regard marriage as a part of the capitalist system of ownership and exploitation. For those feminists, the institution of marriage is, to borrow a phrase from the 20th century radical Max Eastman, "a gauche intrusion on the part of the state and society into the intimacies of private romance."[215]

For such women, stable relationships are difficult to maintain. After all, the belief that one is sleeping with the enemy, so to speak, is not conducive to a healthy relationship. That is why women who adopt these views often end up belligerent, bitter, and lonely.

Luckily, most Muslim women are not that far gone. Yet even narratives that occupy a place lower on that scale are pernicious.

Narratives that celebrate barren, nihilistic distractions at the expense of family and authentic life-sustaining happiness, narratives that swindle women into thinking that wasting their youth and slaving away at some meaningless desk job is the peak of achievement, narratives that deceive women into believing that a suitable partner will be readily available whenever they choose to settle down all burst when they come in contact with reality and mess up the lives of the women who uphold them.

When I ask the students I teach at university (who are predominantly female) about the optimal age to get married, they unanimously state that the optimal age for a woman to do so is close to thirty. When I ask why, they say that a woman must focus on her career first. They believe that if a woman is successful in her career, it improves her prospects. What these young women do not grasp is that their rationale works for men, because the desirability of men hinges predominantly on their ability to provide. The same reasoning does not hold for women because a woman's desirability in the sexual marketplace is predicated on her youth and fertility. A woman doesn't have time to strike out, tarry about, play the field, fool around, and "discover herself," because by the time she hits thirty she will have already lost ninety percent of her ovarian eggs as shown in a recent study from the University of St. Andrews and Edinbrugh University.[216] This is the wall. It cannot be bargained or bamboozled – even with copious application of makeup.

But what about better jobs and higher degrees? Don't they improve a woman's eligibility? No, quite the opposite, in fact. As psychologist Dr. Helen Smith observed in her book, *Men on Strike*, education and earning power actually *shrink* a woman's acceptable dating pool. That is because women, unlike men, tend to be hypergamous – they seek men of equal or higher socio-economic status. In other words, they marry up. So as a woman ascends the socioeconomic hierarchy, she finds fewer men attractive as eligible marriage prospects.[217]

Moreover, the male-centered careers that young women are being prodded to covet are often soul-crushing jobs in pressure cooker environments. Women, who according to Dr. Rita Valentino from the Children's

Hospital of Philadelphia, are twice as vulnerable as men to stress-related disorders and more prone to emotional stress[218], become overwhelmed under these circumstances. Furthermore, because of the time commitments these jobs require, women who work in these competitive settings often have difficulty maintaining proper work-life balance. They end up unable to sustain a relationship, or their relationships fall into shambles – their personal lives reduced to a vain sacrifice on the altar of material ambition. They might look like the poster image of the strong, independent woman on the outside, but under the surface their lives are an unenviable mess.

In his aptly named book *Bleak House*, Charles Dickens presents us with the character of Mrs. Jellyby. A mother and a philanthropist, she obsesses about the plight of the natives in Africa while neglecting her home, spouse, and children. Despite the worthiness of her adopted cause, Dickens does not present her as a character worthy of admiration. On the contrary, she engenders ridicule, if not contempt. Dickens understood that charity, as the proverb says, begins at home. But since then, conventional wisdom has undergone a gnostic reversal. Now a character like Mrs. Jellyby would be celebrated as a successful woman, worthy of being the main protagonist in a Netflix series. Women who have "soul-conflicts" instead of children are put on a pedestal, while housewives are presented as "desperate."

Speaking of which, during my time teaching adult clients, the happiest women I have come across were always the housewives. Do not be fooled by what Hollywood tells you: these women were not desperate. On the contrary, they were quite savvy. As Richard M. Weaver pointed out about women in the world's *ancien régime*, these women understood that power does not lie in "imitativeness, exhibitionism, and cheap bids for attention" but in being loyal to what they are. Despite being educated and capable of finding a decent job, they made the conscious choice to focus on raising their children. They understood that motherhood was not a form of biological drudgery that squanders a woman's true potential. On the contrary, channeling one's energy into raising a human being was far more meaningful – and rewarding – than anything they would otherwise do. And because they did not try – in vain – to juggle between their work and their family, they had time for themselves, time to breathe. Hence, they retained some of the vigor of youth, whereas their displaced pop-culture-celebrated career-focused counterparts who labor without heart and without incentive had all but lost theirs.

I am not making the case that women should not seek higher degrees. I come from a family of highly educated women. I believe an educated mother can make better choices in raising her children. But it is one thing for a woman to finish her bachelor's degree before getting married. It is another thing entirely to postpone marriage, or forego it altogether, in favor of climbing the corporate ladder, because the longer she waits, the less likely she is to find a suitable partner to stand by her side through life's travails.

It is human nature not to wish unalloycd happiness to those who choose to live differently than we do. As such, Muslims love to point out, with some degree of *schadenfreude*, that relationship dynamics in the West are dysfunctional whereas marital relationships in the Muslim world are much more stable. Judging by current trends, and seeing the aforementioned *dangerous narratives* manifested before me in my generation, I would wager that this will all soon take a turn for the worse. When the present generation, which has internalized these narratives, hits middle age, we shall see the calamitous consequences this has on individuals, on families, and on society. We can already see one of these consequences in the closing of the Muslim womb. As noted by economist David P. Goldman in his book *How Civilizations Die*, fertility in the Muslim world is already falling two to three times faster than the world average. [219] This will lead to a demographic implosion that will wreck havoc on the fledgling economies of the Muslim world. In addition to this, we will also start seeing the same problems that plague western societies including high divorce rates, low marriage rates, and the appearance of single parent households on the home front – along with all the concomitant social and economic issues.

It is not the *hijab*, *burqa*, and other sartorial concerns that Muslim women need to defy. It is the feminist tropes underlying virtually every movie that are hurrying them to perdition and predisposing them to an abject, lonesome existence marked by emptiness, frustration, general anxiety, and cat hair.

Chapter 14

Prudes, Nudes, and Dangerous Attitudes

The imam, perched on the pulpit, was fuming.

People all around the mosque were squatting down on the carpets. They wiggled their toes and stared into space. They were waiting for the imam to finish shouting out the Friday sermon so they could carry on with their lives. Meanwhile, the imam railed. Was he lamenting the state of unemployment or education in the Muslim world? Was he angry at the atrocities being committed in the name of Islam? No. Only one topic could get the imam so riled up: scantily-clad women. The imam was going into an epileptic fit because of skinny jeans and the occasional mini skirt.

Growing up in the Muslim world, I heard that sermon multiple times. It was a recurring theme. Whether on Friday sermons or on talk shows, one can see religious men talking about clothes with so much gusto they make the guys on *Queer Eye* seem apathetic about fashion.

When Sayyid Qutb, the forefather of Islamist thought, went to the United States, one of the key points that he fixated on was the intermingling of the sexes and the flagrant sexuality displayed by people there. Keep in mind that Qutb's trip did not take place in the present day or in the freewheeling sixties. It took place in 1948 in Greeley, Colorado, a small conservative town in which even alcohol was illegal.

Here is what Qutb had to say about American women:

> The American girl is well acquainted with her body's seductive capacity. She knows it lies in the face, and in expressive eyes, and thirsty lips. She knows seductiveness lies in the round breasts, the full buttocks, and in the shapely thighs, sleek legs… and in clothes… that reveal the temptations of the body.[220]

American men did not escape his scrutiny either:

> The American boy knows well that the wide, strapping chest is the lure that cannot be

denied by any girl, and that her dreams do not fall upon anyone as much as they fall upon the cowboys… And *Look Magazine* ran a survey of several girls of different ages and levels of education and classes around what it called "ox muscles" and the overwhelming majority declared their open attraction for boys with ox muscles![221]

Qutb's description, with its sexual overtones and its undercurrent of disdain and resentment, bears a striking resemblance to passages on the internet written by sexually frustrated individuals who identify as "involuntary celibates" or "incels." Qutb claims he was observing as part of a "close study" of American society. Judging by his choice of words, though, I would say he was not observing as much as he was pining.

Take this passage for example, in which Qutb describes an innocent dance at a church club:

… the dance floor was replete with tapping feet, enticing legs, arms wrapped around waists, lips pressed to lips, and chests pressed to chests. The atmosphere was full of desire.[222]

Reading this passage, one can imagine Qutb, a lanky, taciturn figure standing there awkwardly in the corner of the room, gawking at the pretty girls, wistful yet at the same time supercilious, wishing that he was partaking in the merriment while placating himself with feelings of superiority because he was not. The dance floor may have been full of desire, but I would wager, so was Qutb.

Qutb framed his jaundiced "observations" as a matter of morality and community ethics, but it was really about sexual frustration.

Muslims, just like Qutb, are sexually starved. Recently, a ballerina was sexually assaulted by four men in Istanbul. Could have happened anywhere, if it were not for the fact that the ballerina in question was a metal statue. Though she was a bit cold, to say the least, the four grown men could not resist her skimpy outfit and seductive pose.[223] A look at web search data released by Google reaffirms what is made obvious by anecdotal evidence. Six out of the top eight porn consuming countries in the world are Muslim majority states. Pakistan tops the list, while Egypt, Iran, Morocco, Saudi Arabia, and Turkey come in at second, fourth, fifth, seventh, and eighth place respectively.[224]

Why?

Because the Muslim world is stiflingly puritanical. Any sexual activity outside marriage, even masturbation, is a grave sin. So are kissing, dating, and flirting. One imam pontificated, with sanctimony to rival Savonarola's, that even the act of secretly harboring feelings towards a classmate constitutes adultery. As noted by Raphael Patai in his book *The Arab Mind*, rather than steering young people away from sex, these narratives "have the effect of making sex a prime mental preoccupation in the Arab world. The very taboo of sex creates a kind of fixation on the subject."[225]

"But that's not a problem," sayeth the Muslim imams in response to that conundrum. "Just get married."

And there lies the rub.

For many Muslims nowadays, marriage is not accessible. In Islam, getting married is supposed to be easy. All you need are two witnesses. To say Muslims have complicated matters is an understatement. The whole process is now dominated by appearances and conspicuous consumption. It used to be that all a potential groom needed was a stable job and a modest roof over his head. But in the age of Instagram, where people are constantly bombarded with pictures of those living ostentatious lifestyles, that is no longer enough. Now a potential groom must have a nice house, a nice car, and a well-paying job. He must also be able to afford an expensive ring, an extravagant wedding, and an exotic honeymoon. Not to mention, of course, a sizeable dowry to the bride's parents.

Such expectations, previously the concern of the oil-rich and decadent, have trickled down the socio-economic ladder. Now even families of modest means are partaking in this arms race of the vanities. And it is not the people getting married who bring down these obligations upon themselves; the culprits are often the couple's parents. Because for them, a large dowry, a lavish wedding, and a big rock are a license for braggadocio.

This trend has had serious social consequences. For the majority of young Muslim men, marriage has become prohibitively expensive and thus no longer feasible until their mid-thirties, if at all.

While Muslim women are not burdened with the financial expectations foisted on their male counterparts, they are nonetheless affected by this trend. The dearth of financially viable male partners has led to a proportional boom in sad single cat ladies who edge closer to infertility without being able to land themselves a husband.

So young hormone-ridden Muslims are stuck between a Scylla and a Charybdis. They can either go against their own biology and suppress their natural desires well into their thirties and forties, or they can break one of the key injunctions in their faith and engage in sexual relationships outside the bounds of marriage.

Both paths bring their own sets of problems. For those who go down the route of open-ended abstinence, suppression of natural sexual impulses over an extended period can pervert said impulses. One need only look at the rampant sexual abuse scandals in the Catholic Church to see what happens when celibacy is imposed on young men. Worse still, it could lead frustrated individuals to give up on life. The phenomenon of suicide bombers is often blamed on religious schools, radical clerics, or socioeconomic conditions. I believe there is a much simpler explanation – or at least trigger. Borrowing a page from Freud, I propose that it is indeed about sex. I'd wager that if young Muslim men had access to sex, there would be far fewer people willing to detonate themselves.

As for those who disregard religious prohibition on premarital sex, that group opens themselves up to a different kind of problem. A believer cannot break God's law without also giving up a part of his identity – and his conviction. For it is not in a believer's best interest for Islam to be true when he is actively engaged in flouting its commandments. As a way to cope with the guilt, their belief in the sacred turns into cynical nihilism.

The issue of sexuality in the Muslim world is endemic in scope and serious in consequence. Yet the Muslim religious community has not addressed it, let alone offered any solutions to this problem. This intellectual lethargy stems from a *dangerous narrative*, one that purports that early Muslims manifested the kind of sexual puritanism and conservatism that is expected of young Muslims today. If they could pull it off, it is assumed, then certainly Muslims today can pull it off too. The responsibility for failing to do so lies squarely on this generation of Muslims.

This *dangerous narrative* is one that I find particularly vexing because of the egregious intellectual dishonesty required to peddle it. Any honest reading of early Islamic history shows that sexual restrictions in early Muslim societies were, in fact, more lax than those

Muslims are expected to observe today. As historian Daniel Pipes notes, in Muslim societies, sexual satisfaction – for both men and women – was seen as a path to a "harmonious social order and a flourishing civilization."[226]

That is *not* to say that early Muslims were sexual libertines or that they did not observe religious commandants regarding sex. They had a higher degree of sexual propriety. However, they had many more outlets for their sexuality than are available in today's Muslim societies. They could get married young, in their teens and early twenties, without having to fulfil a tall order of outrageous material prerequisites. They could marry four wives simultaneously. They were also permitted to have sex with concubines.[a]

Islam, ever the pragmatic religion, understands the human condition. Though it sets limitations on acceptable sexual behavior, it also sanctions multiple channels to ease those limitations.

---

[a] This passage might conjure in the reader's mind images of what one might expect takes place at the Playboy Mansion. However, in reality it wasn't anything like that. While polygamy and concubinage were permitted in Islam, they were nonetheless highly regulated. For example, men who took multiple wives had to provide a separate home for each one. Also, it's worth noting here that while Islam allows polygamy, it clearly states that it is better to be monogamous.

Muslims nowadays have closed every one of those channels. Polygamy is frowned upon in most Muslim societies, concubinage has been abolished, and loopholes like "pleasure marriages" (*nikah mut'a*) are deemed unlawful by the majority of modern-day Muslims. Even monogamous marriage, the go-to be-all-end-all solution offered by religious figures, is practically inaccessible for most men at their sexual prime.

Muslims have thus been barred from every channel through which they could satisfy their natural desires and are left solely with the limitations imposed upon them.

The reason there has not been a public outcry in the Muslim world demanding religious authorities to step up and improvise credible solutions is that the majority of Muslims are ignorant of the aforementioned allowances that were afforded to their forefathers. You never hear about concubines or the historical origins of pleasure marriages in a Friday sermon. Religious authorities deliberately skip those parts. You never hear the faintest mention of the sensual pleasures that Muhammad and his companions indulged in.[a] You just hear about the eternal

---

[a] This statement is not meant to be derogatory but is simply a matter of fact. Muhammad and his companions indulged in and enjoyed sex in all ways that it was religiously permissible and socially acceptable for them to do so. They weren't different in that regard from Abraham, Jacob, Moses, Hosea, Saul,

hellfire awaiting Abdullah for texting his crush or spanking his monkey.

These Muslims, who have been fed a doctored version of their history, develop the assumption that what religious society expects from them is reasonable and is in line with Islam. So when they fail to live up to this concocted standard, they attribute their failure to personal weakness.

I am not pointing out historical reality in defense of concubinage, or pleasure marriages, or any particular allowance that was available during Islam's formative years. I am not laying the ground to offer a solution either. I am not a trained theologian, and hence I am in no position to improvise solutions to such a matter. However, I seek to emphasize that we do have a problem when it comes to sexuality in the Muslim world, and abstinence is not a realistic solution. If even early Muslims, whom we are repeatedly taught are the paradigms of virtue and willpower, could not abstain from sex for the duration of a trip while in the presence of the Prophet and had to be allowed to engage in temporary marriages, it is unreasonable to expect

---

David, and Solomon who had either multiple wives, multiple concubines, or both.

young Muslims in today's hypersexualized world to abstain from sex for decades.

Religious authorities need to improvise on this issue and offer solutions that take into account present realities. Solutions like "just get married" or "marry young" are bromides divorced from the facts on the ground.[a]

Failure to do so will cause young Muslims to develop a wide range of mental and behavioral problems. In the long run, it will even lead people to drift away from the religion itself. When a religion becomes unpracticable and disconnected from reality, people lose faith in it over time.

---

[a] Just to clarify, these solutions are not inherently bad. The problem is that without dealing with the obstacles and barriers in modern Muslim societies that prevent young Muslim couples from getting married, these solutions remain unworkable.

Chapter 15

Islam and Government

Islam originated at the beginning of the 7th century. From that time on, over the span of nearly one thousand four hundred years, Muslims enjoyed several periods of unrivaled prosperity. The leaders who presided over these epochs loom large over our collective memory. Omar, Ali, Harun al-Rashid, Saladin, Mehmet the Conqueror, Suleiman the Magnificent – for Muslims these figures, giants among men, represent lodestars of meritorious conduct and good leadership.

The veneration of these leaders and the romanticizing of those epochs have led some Muslims to believe that the answer for all of today's predicaments can be found within Islamic history.

That is a *dangerous narrative*, because Islamic history does not provide us with a suitable roadmap for moving forward.

It suggests that all power should flow directly from the leader and it casts him as a pure-hearted savior rather than a mere administrator. That is why so many Muslims today pin their hope on the emergence of such a messianic figure – someone pure and just who will steer us through our sea of troubles into a new Golden Age.

This notion is problematic on several fronts. To begin with, even if a leader has good intentions, that is not a guarantee that he will be competent.

Purity of heart and personal wisdom are no longer sufficient to make sense of, much less revamp, the complex systems in today's world. Muhammad could be depended on to give wise council whether the matter at hand was martial, marital, economic, or environmental. Seventh century Arabia was a simpler place.

Furthermore, leaders can also become corrupt; they can lose touch with the world; they can lose their grip on sanity; and they can be killed. To pin a country's destiny on a thing so frail is foolish.

But most importantly, when a leader comes to power, his actions can only be as good as the ideas and the narratives lying around. One time, I was having a conversation in which I asked the following question: "What would you do if you were president?" She said the first thing she would do is get the smartest people in each field to come up with a good system.

Good thing it was all theoretical, because that is a recipe for a coup d'etat. When you come to power, there is no time to fish around for good systems. As Rousseau pointed out, the formation of laws leaves the state vulnerable. In times of peace and plenty, one can afford to do that, but in unstable countries like those in the Middle East, one does not have that luxury, you cannot go through a process of trial and error. You must have effective ideas and systems ready to be put in place. If you do not, you will be forced to use the defective systems already in place, and any good coming from the new government will be bound by that fact, irrespective of who leads it.

This brings me to the following point: what maintains political entities and determines how well they function in the long run are not their leaders but their institutions and, by extension, the narratives they are built upon. Times of war aside, the impact of institutions supersedes that of leaders. In fact, institutions, as Montesquieu noted, even mold the rulers themselves.[227] Good institutional arrangements force a leader to act in a decent manner even if he is not a decent person morally.

Take the United States for example. In two hundred and fifty years, they have never had a civil war over the issue of succession. This was not a stroke of good luck nor, was it due to the character of those who held office. It is laws and institutions that ensure a smooth transition of power every election cycle and preclude someone from usurping the presidency.

President Donald Trump openly expressed his admiration when China got rid of presidential term limits. He even mused that maybe America too should "give that a shot."[228] He would probably like nothing better than to be *dictator perpetuo*, like all the autocrats he admires. But that is not going to happen because of the established laws and institutions in place.

The second issue with that narrative is its legacy of autocratic rule. When all the great leaders in one's history were autocrats, it is easy to be well-disposed to despotism.

Muslims, however, do not realize that the success of an autocratic government under a good king does not make the case for an autocratic system. As noted by Rousseau, to see such a system by itself, "we must look at it under princes who are incompetent or wicked."[229]

This is why over the long run, a good political system is not one that allows a great leader to achieve his maximum potential. It is one that strikes the proper balance between empowering leaders while simultaneously restraining them. Such a system limits the good that can be done, but it also mitigates the damage that can be caused.

There is also the following psychological consideration. Autocratic systems impair the psyche of the general populace. As noted by Alexis de Tocqueville, an autocratic system extends "its arms over the entire society with a network of small, complicated, minute, and uniform rules." It "enervates" a nation and turns its citizens into "a flock of timid and industrious animals."[230] After all, as Eric Hoffer writes in his book, *The Ordeal of Change*, "absolute power produces not a society but a menagerie," since even under a "benevolent despot who sees himself as a shepherd," the people are forced to exhibit "the submissiveness of sheep."[231] This might explain why the various Muslim empires all slipped into torpor once they became well established.

So Islamic history does not provide us with the best template to emulate, but what about Islam itself? Muslims maintain that Islam furnishes us with the answer in the concept of *shura*.

Islam does indeed prescribe *shura*. Unfortunately, it does not go into details as to what it means by *shura*. All we know is that it means "consultation." Great. Now what? How do you elect a leader? Who is eligible for voting? Does everyone's opinion carry equal weight? Should there be a term limit on elected office, and if so how long should it be? Should the leader be able act out his will on any matter, or should his sphere of authority be limited? What governing bodies should there be besides the head of state? Are they appointed by and answerable to him, or does he have to answer to them? What happens when the leader is tyrannical or deranged? Should he be overthrown, and if so what is the mechanism to do so?

And forget about the political structure for a moment. What about the laws governing the state? What should they be based on? Should laws be based on religion? If so, who determines which interpretation of religion should be used in drafting laws? Islam does not have a priesthood, so who determines if laws are based on Islamic principles? Strike that, who is going to determine what constitutes Islamic principles in the first place?

And what about taxes and tariffs and healthcare and education? Should we adopt a socialist model or a capitalist one?

These are all basic questions that Islam unfortunately does not answer. As noted by Mustafa Akyol, "Muslim scripture is almost silent on the fundamental issues of politics" and so was Muhammad who "left neither a political heir nor an institution … [to] govern in his absence."[232] There is no prescription in Islam on the best form of governance beyond the mere hint that it should involve consultation. The historical institution known as the Caliphate that was formed after the Prophet's death was in fact based on the political norms of 7th century Arabia not on any divine mandate.

Is it divine oversight? No. I believe that God never prescribed the optimal political system because had he done so Muslims would have been indomitable. Even while plagued with internal conflict and continuous succession crises, Muslims still managed to establish one of the largest and greatest empires that the world has ever seen, larger even than Rome at its zenith. Imagine how powerful they would have been if they had a political system that ensured that only the most meritorious held the reins of power and established a system for succession that did not involve civil war and the occasional fratricide. Muslims would have conquered the world.

God never meant for the world to be homogeneous; he says so in the Quran, "...had Allah willed, He would have made you one nation, but [He intended] to test you in what He has given you; so race to [all that is] good. To Allah is your return all together, and He will [then] inform you concerning that over which you used to differ." (5:48) That is why when it comes to having a good political system, we have been left to our devices. We do not have a ready-to-be-applied God-certified blueprint. Muslims need to come to terms with that.

But just because we do not have an agreed-upon model for an Islamic state in our history and in our religion does not mean that we can turn blindly to the West for answers either. The importation of certain Western political concepts, like nationalism and the nation state as a model of sovereignty, has been nothing short of catastrophic in the Muslim world. The fragmentation of the Muslim world into territorial units where discord could be constructed and encouraged is rooted in those ideas.

Even democracy, is not the silver bullet it is hailed out to be. As noted by Yuval Noah Harari in his book, *21 Lessons for the 21st Century*, holding general elections in places like Iraq, Afghanistan, and Congo does not "magically turn these places into sunnier versions of Denmark." [233] There are many third world countries, including Lebanon, my country of birth, that do have free elections and have had free elections for decades, yet they show no signs whatsoever of metamorphosing into a Western European country or a Baltic state.

That is because democracy requires preconditions that the Muslim world lacks. As noted by Eric Hoffer, freedom requires that a country at least be able to function adequately in normal times without the need for unanimity.[234] In Lebanon, the government could not even arrange for the trash to get picked up for several years. That is not a society fit for freedom.

Furthermore, for democracy to work, "a society needs a large measure of affluence... [and] it must be able to afford the waste inherent in a riot of trial and error."[235] Take China for example. I do not think its phenomenal growth and modernization would have been possible if the government was more democratic and less centralized, as the majority of its citizens are too poor and too unskilled.

They are not an untapped well of constructive social energies. Giving them free rein to pursue their own initiatives and interests would only lead to social chaos and mayhem. Perhaps in the future, a liberal democracy would be in China's favor, but not at the moment.

So back to the issue of a suitable form of government, we do not have prepackaged, ready-made answers. We have to find our own answers. We need a system where good governance does not rest solely on having a good leader – as has traditionally been the case in Muslim states. Good governance should be guaranteed by institutional arrangements that force leaders to be good even when they are not.

If Muslims want to live in a democracy and enjoy a high standard of living, then they also need a system that can afford waste. For that, Muslims need to transcend their national and ethnic identities so that the disparate nations of the Muslim world can reintegrate into an economically sustainable entity.

And even when Muslims do find the answer, implementing it will be a challenge in itself because they would have to work within the system. Political organization is something that develops over time. Any attempt to impose it by force, no matter how lofty its ideals, would end up being a messy, bloody affair. Whoever comes to power in that manner will always end up oppressing those he is supposed to deliver.

The transformational process will be very slow. It might take generations to see its fruits. It is a depressing thought, one outweighed only by the fact that if Muslims do nothing, if they keep insisting that they have all the answers, then their situation will only become worse and they will keep wondering how people who supposedly have all the answers could be living in such a wretched state.

Chapter 16
Conclusion

This book looks at the mind-forged manacles that hold Muslims back. It does not look, however, at the structural elements affecting how they think and act. In doing so, one might come under the impression that I lay the blame entirely on behavioral choices and a defective culture.

I do not. I am aware of the impact that structures have. So why do I focus on one and ignore the other?

Because for most of us, changing major structural elements in our society is not within our power. We do not have the power to change the laws, the institutions, the political structure, or the socio-economic conditions. But we can change ourselves. I do not subscribe to the Watsonian view that man is nothing but a product of his environment. I believe instead in the Quranic position that states, "God does not change the condition of a people until they change what is in themselves." (13:11)

Change-by-narratives is a slow process, but once narratives gain momentum, once they take root in the multitude, they can change the world dramatically. As Georg Wilhelm Friedrich Hegel once said, "Once the world of ideas has been transformed, reality cannot hold out for long." Look at the European Union. If you told any person living on the European continent a hundred years ago that Europeans should put aside their differences and band together as one power, he would have told you it is impossible. Europe is strewn with the bones of those who perished in its countless wars. There is too much history, too much enmity, too much bad blood to overcome.

By they did overcome it. Once they embraced the narrative that despite local differences they are one people, with one heritage, a united Europe was made possible. One of my Spanish students once told me that as soon as she crosses from Turkey into Bulgaria and sees the flag of the European Union at the border crossing, she feels at home. For her, all the EU is home.

Israel did it as well. They started with no land, just a diaspora. Until Theodore Herzl reimagined the ancient religious community as a nation. Once that narrative took hold in that community, the State of Israel became *fait accompli*.

But where do such narratives come from? How would the Muslim world overcome their *dangerous narratives* and substitute them with constructive ones?

One thing is certain, these narratives are not a grassroots affair – not at the inception stage at least. They won't come from the masses. New narratives are never put forth or propagated by the majority who, as the famous French social psychologist Gustave Le Bon pointed out, have neither the discipline nor the forethought required for the task. [236] Hence it always falls upon a vocal and educated minority, an intellectual aristocracy so to speak, to lead the way. The masses just follow suit.

So what Muslims need are Herzls of their own – a vigorous intelligentsia. Not the ivory tower academics who occupy positions of power within the current establishment. Those fulfill the same role as the scribes of Sumer, the literati of Egypt, the brahmins of India, the mandarins of China, the rabbis of Judea, and the clerks of the Catholic

Church in the sense that they all prop the status quo. Ensconced in their bureaucratic niche, they hold no grievances and dream no dreams.

No, the new Muslim intellectual vanguard will be born from the ranks of a dispossessed educated elite. As economic development in the Muslim world fails to keep up with the rapid expansion of tertiary education, an increasing number of people are finding the way for purposeful action and privileged rank to be blocked. Their dissatisfaction mixed with the vision and ability commensurate with their education will act as an impetus for change and drive them to take current narratives head-on. I use the terminology of siege warfare because, indeed, as Dutch historian Rutger Bregman pointed out, "A worldview is not a Lego set where a block is added here, removed there. It's a fortress that is defended tooth and nail, with all possible reinforcements, until the pressure becomes so overpowering that the walls cave in."[237]

But Muslims need to be wary of two kinds of easy fixes: imitation and innovation. Refashioning the Muslim world into a carbon copy of the West is not the answer. First it would be unimplementable as any attempt to do so would require the use of force. The resulting authoritarian regime would be nothing like the model that it set out to emulate. Second, even if it were possible, it would not be desirable. It would only substitute one set of *dangerous narratives* with another, for – make no mistake – the West also suffers from a deep malaise stemming from its own *dangerous narratives*. That is why, despite producing a cornucopia for itself, Western industrialized countries have been shown in numerous cross-cultural studies to be "afflicted with some of the highest rates of depression, schizophrenia, poor health, anxiety, and chronic loneliness in human history."[238]

Likewise, innovation untempered by learning and wisdom is dangerous. The dominant narratives in the Muslim world will be challenged in the years to come. But in the ranks of those who will throw down the gauntlet, there will be a lot of false prophets. There will also be people who will spurn inherited wisdom in favor of their own private stock of reason, not realizing how limited that stock is. In doing so, they will undermine or discredit social norms and institutions that actually serve a valuable function. Their high-flown narratives might be novel in this part of the world, but they would not be better. They would promise blessings but bring down calamities.

At the turn of the 20th century, the westernized literary classes were dissatisfied with the state of affairs in the ailing Ottoman Empire. They could have sought to reform it. It would have been a monumental task, but doable nonetheless. In that imperial state they had, borrowing a phrase from Edmund Burke, "the foundations of a noble and venerable castle."[239] But in their hubris, they sought to discard all the vestiges of the established order, in religion, in polity, in laws, and in manners. In doing so, they precipitated the demise of an Empire that Michel de Montaigne, one of the most prominent French philosophers during the Renaissance, once described as "the strongest state" in the world.[240] Now modern Turkey is but a shadow of its *ancien régime*, and its status as a regional power exists not because of the changes those upstarts imposed on it a hundred years ago but in spite of them.

In coming up with new narratives, Muslims need to adopt a judicious rather than a contrarian mindset. In other words, they need to accept that the right way *might* be opposite to what everyone thinks, not that it *must* be opposite to what everyone thinks. Hence they should abide the middle path between imitation and innovation. They do need to learn from the experience of others, and sometimes they should challenge conventional wisdom when that wisdom is not true to its name. But they also need to retain the aspects of their cultural and spiritual inheritance that are worthy of retaining.

This is the kind of revolution that the Muslim world needs; not a revolution marked by the number of protesters or the power of arms but one distinguished by the power of its ideas. Only such a revolution can bring forth a "spring."

Until then, Muslims are fated to suffer an endless winter of discontent. And for that, they only have themselves to blame. As Shakespeare put it, the fault lies not in our stars, but in ourselves – and in our narratives – that we are underlings.

NOTES

[1] Kindersley, Dorling. *The Philosophy Book: Big Ideas Simply Explained*. DK Publishing, 2017.

[2] UNICEF. 'Five Things You Didn't Know About Female Genital Mutilation/Cutting.' UNICEF Connect. August 24, 2018. Accessed October 13, 2018. https://blogs.unicef.org/blog/five-things-you-didnt-know-about-female-genital-mutilationcutting-2/.

[3] Drum, Kevin. 'Female Genital Mutilation Is Not a Uniquely Muslim Problem.' Mother Jones, June 24, 2017. www.motherjones.com/kevin-drum/2016/02/female-genital-mutilation-not-uniquely-muslim-problem/.

[4] Akyol, Mustafa. *Islam without Extremes: A Muslim Case for Liberty*. New York: W.W. Norton & Company, 2013.

[5] Esposito, John L. *What Everyone Needs to Know About Islam* (2nd edn). Oxford University Press, 2011.

[6] 'Egypt Mufti Says Female Circumcision Forbidden.' Reuters. June 24, 2007. Accessed October 13, 2018. www.reuters.com/article/idUSL24694871.

7 Miller, Yvette Alt. 'Albanian Muslims Who Sheltered Jews.' Aishcom. March 3, 2018. Accessed October 13, 2018. www.aish.com/ho/p/Albanian-Muslims-who-Sheltered-Jews.html.

8 Haines, Gavin. 'Mapped: The World's Most (and Least) Free Countries.' *The Telegraph*. May 24, 2016. Accessed July 22, 2019. www.telegraph.co.uk/travel/news/the-worlds-most-authoritarian-destinations/.

9 'Economy of the Organisation of Islamic Cooperation.' Wikipedia. July 15, 2019. Accessed July 22, 2019. https://en.wikipedia.org/wiki/Economy_of_the_Organisation_of_Islamic_Cooperation.

10 'Higher Education: Governance, Innovation and Employability.' ISESCO Headquarters, Rabat, Morocco, December 2014. www.isesco.org.ma/7cimesrs/doc/en/2-4VE.pdf.

11 'Nearly 40% of Muslim World's Population Unable Read or Write: IINA Report.' UNA. January 14, 2015. Accessed July 22, 2019. www.iinanews.com/page/public/report.aspx?id=10377#.XTW6NPIzaUk.

12 Khan, Taimur. 'Muslim Countries Have Highest Rates of Suicide, Murder, Rape and Mental Health Problems.' *The National*. August 8, 2017. Accessed July 22, 2019. www.thenational.ae/world/muslim-countries-have-highest-rates-of-suicide-murder-rape-and-mental-health-problems-1.618038.

13 Lipka, Michael. 'Muslims and Islam: Key Findings in the U.S. and Around the World.' Pew Research Center. August

9, 2017. Accessed October 27, 2018.
www.pewresearch.org/fact-tank/2017/08/09/muslims-and-i
slam-key-findings-in-the-u-s-and-around-the-world/.

[14] *Ibid.*

[15] Liu, Joseph. 'The Future of the Global Muslim
Population.' Pew Research Center's Religion & Public Life
Project. October 22, 2018. Accessed October 27, 2018.
www.pewforum.org/2011/01/27/the-future-of-the-global-m
uslim-population/.

[16] DiChristopher, Tom. 'Saudi Crown Prince Threatens to
Develop a Nuke as Kingdom Seeks Foreign Nuclear
Technology.' CNBC. March 15, 2018. Accessed October 13,
2018.
www.cnbc.com/2018/03/15/saudi-crown-prince-threatens-t
o-build-nuke-as-kingdom-seeks-nuclear-tech.html.

[17] Smyth, Patrick. 'The War to End All War.' *The Irish
Times*. May 14, 2014. Accessed October 13, 2018.
www.irishtimes.com/culture/heritage/the-war-to-end-all-wa
r-1.1786559.

[18] 'International Propagation of Salafism and Wahhabism.'
Wikipedia. July 7, 2019. Accessed July 22, 2019.
https://en.wikipedia.org/wiki/International_propagation_of
_Salafism_and_Wahhabism.

[19] 'Sykes–Picot Agreement.' Wikipedia. September 17,
2018. Accessed October 13, 2018.
https://en.wikipedia.org/wiki/Sykes–Picot_Agreement.

[20] 'Balfour Declaration.' Wikipedia. October 07, 2018.
Accessed October 13, 2018.
https://en.wikipedia.org/wiki/Balfour_Declaration.

21 Akyol, Mustafa. *Islam without Extremes: a Muslim Case for Liberty*. New York: W.W. Norton & Company, 2013.

22 Hoffer, Eric. *TRUE BELIEVER: Thoughts on the Nature of Mass Movements*. S.l.: HARPERCOLLINS, 2019.

23 Ibid.

24 Harris, Sam, and Maajid Nawaz. *Islam and the Future of Tolerance: a Dialogue*. Cambridge, MA: Harvard University Press, 2015.

25 Peterson, Jordan B. *12 Rules for Life: An Antidote for Chaos*. London: Allen Lane, 2018.

26 Rousseau, Jean-Jacques. *The Social Contract*. 2010, in the version translated by Jonathan Bennett presented at www.earlymoderntexts.com

27 Nietzsche, Friedrich. *Thus Spoke Zarathustra*. Logos Publishing, 2017.

28 Brown, Jonathan. *Misquoting Muhammad: The Challenge and Choices of Interpreting the Prophets Legacy*. London: Oneworld, 2016.

29 Islamweb. Accessed September 22, 2018. http://fatwa.islamweb.net/fatwa/index.php?page=showfatwa&Option=FatwaId&Id=219475.

30 Aslan, Reza. *No God but God: The Origins and Evolution of Islam*. New York: Ember, 2012.

31 Turner, Bryan. 'Max Weber and the Sociology of Islam.' *Revue Internationale De Philosophie* 276, no. 2 (2016): 213-229. www.cairn.info/revue-revue-internationale-de-philosophie-2016-2-page-213.html.

32 Harris, Sam, and Maajid Nawaz. *Islam and the Future of Tolerance a Dialogue*. Cambridge, MA: Harvard University Press, 2015.

33 Aslan, Reza. *No God but God: The Origins and Evolution of Islam*. New York: Ember, 2012.

34 Ibid.

35 Brown, Jonathan A. C. *Misquoting Muhammad: The Challenge and Choices of Interpreting the Prophets Legacy*. London: Oneworld, 2014.

36 Esposito, John L. *What Everyone Needs to Know about Islam (2nd Edition)*. Oxford University Press, 2011.

37 Russell, Bertrand. *Why I Am Not a Christian: And Other Essays on Religion and Related Subjects*. New York: Simon & Schuster, 1996.

38 Osborne, Samuel. 'Someone Analysed the Bible and Quran to See Which Is More Violent.' *The Independent*. December 04, 2016. Accessed November 10, 2018. www.independent.co.uk/arts-entertainment/books/violence-more-common-in-bible-than-quran-text-analysis-reveals-a6863381.html.

39 Nydell, Margaret K. *Understanding Arabs: A Contemporary Guide to Arab Society*. Boston: Intercultural Press, an Imprint of Nicholas Brealey Publishing, 2014.

40 Salama, Samir. 'Muslims Observe Prophet's Birthday Today.' Arts Culture – Gulf News. Gulf News, October 29, 2018. https://gulfnews.com/entertainment/arts-culture/muslims-observe-prophets-birthday-today-1.1642990.

41 Aslan, Reza. *No God but God: The Origins and Evolution of Islam*. New York: Ember, 2012.

42 Voltaire. *Treatise on Tolerance*. 2018, in the version translated by Jonathan Bennett presented at www.earlymoderntexts.com

43 Ibid.

44 Lewis, Bernard. *What Went Wrong?: Approaches to the Modern History of the Middle East*. New York: Oxford University Press, 2002.

45 Rousseau, Jean-Jacques. *The Social Contract*. 2010, in the version translated by Jonathan Bennett presented at www.earlymoderntexts.com

46 'Theodosian Code.' Accessed November 02, 2018. www.scrollpublishing.com/store/Theodosian-Code.html.

47 Sonin, Konstantin. 'Russia's Economic Stagnation Is Here to Stay by Konstantin Sonin.' Project Syndicate. February 01, 2018. Accessed November 09, 2018. www.project-syndicate.org/commentary/russia-economic-stagnation-structural-reform-by-konstantin-sonin-2018-02?barrier=accesspaylog.

48 'GDP Growth (annual %).' The World Bank. Accessed November 09, 2018. https://data.worldbank.org/indicator/NY.GDP.MKTP.KD.ZG?end=2017&locations=CN&start=2009.

49 Evans, David C., and Mark R. Peattie. *Kaigun: Strategy, Tactics, and Technology in the Imperial Japanese Navy, 1887-1941*. Annapolis: Naval Institute Press, 2012.

50 'Bambatha Rebellion.' Wikipedia. July 28, 2018. Accessed November 13, 2018. https://en.wikipedia.org/wiki/Bambatha_Rebellion.

51 Hobbes, Thomas. *Leviathan*. 2006, in the version translated by Jonathan Bennett presented at www.earlymoderntexts.com

52 Kant, Immanuel. *Toward Perpetual Peace*. 2010, in the version translated by Jonathan Bennett presented at www.earlymoderntexts.com

53 Dalrymple, William. 'William Dalrymple: Mumbai Atrocities Highlight Need for Solution in Kashmir.' *The Guardian*. Guardian News and Media, November 30, 2008. www.theguardian.com/commentisfree/2008/nov/30/mumbai-terror-attacks-india1.

54 'AL-AQSA MOSQUE ADDRESS BY ABU HANIFA AWDA: WE WILL LAY SIEGE TO ROME, TURN WHITE HOUSE BLACK, IMPOSE JIZYA TAX ON LONDON, AND PRAY ON THE SLOPES OF THE ROCKIES AND ANDES.' MEMRI. June 2, 2019. Accessed June 20, 2019. www.memri.org/tv/aqsa-mosque-address-palestinian-sheikh-hanifa-awda-brigade-conquer-world-jerusalem-seat-caliphate.

55 Al-Banna, Hassan. 'Al-Jihad.' Accessed October 26, 2018. https://thequranblog.files.wordpress.com/2008/06/_10_-al-jihad.pdf.

56 '10 Islamic Rules of War.' The Deen Show. Accessed October 25, 2018. www.thedeenshow.com/10-islamic-rules-of-war/.

[57] Quṭb, Sayyid. *Milestones*. Birmingham: Maktabah Booksellers and Publishers, 2006.

[58] Ibid.

[59] Ibid.

[60] Abu Zakaria. *Jesus: Man, Messenger, Messiah*. iERA. 2017.

[61] Gobash, Omar Saif. *Letters to a Young Muslim*. London: Picador, 2018.

[62] Orwell, George. *Homage to Catalonia*. London: Folio Society, 1970.

[63] Aderet, Ofer. 'Testimonies from the Censored Deir Yassin Massacre: "They Piled Bodies and Burned Them."' *Haaretz*. April 24, 2018. Accessed July 17, 2018. www.haaretz.com/israel-news/MAGAZINE-testimonies-from-the-censored-massacre-at-deir-yassin-1.5494094.

[64] 'Killings and Massacres during the 1948 Palestine War.' Wikipedia. September 19, 2018. Accessed September 22, 2018. https://en.wikipedia.org/wiki/Killings_and_massacres_during_the_1948_Palestine_war.

[65] Weiss, Philip. 'A Brief, Unhappy History of Israeli Massacres.' Mondoweiss. April 02, 2018. Accessed September 22, 2018. https://mondoweiss.net/2018/04/unhappy-history-massacres/.

[66] Ofir, Jonathan. '"Barbarism by an Educated and Cultured People" - Dawayima Massacre Was Worse than Deir Yassin.' Mondoweiss. October 30, 2017. Accessed July 17,

2018.
https://mondoweiss.net/2016/02/barbarism-by-an-educated-and-cultured-people-dawayima-massacre-was-worse-than-deir-yassin/.

[67] Cook, Jonathan. 'Nakba Survivors Share Their Stories of Loss and Hope.' *Al Jazeera.* May 19, 2016. Accessed July 17, 2018.
www.aljazeera.com/news/2016/05/nakba-survivors-share-stories-loss-hope-160517094112558.html.

[68] 'Killings and Massacres during the 1948 Palestine War.' Wikipedia. July 14, 2018. Accessed July 17, 2018.
https://en.wikipedia.org/wiki/Killings_and_massacres_during_the_1948_Palestine_war.

[69] Boyle, Francis Anthony. *Palestine, Palestinians, and International Law.* Malaysia: Crescent News, 2007.

[70] 'Hamas: We Never Wanted to Throw Jews in Sea.' Ynetnews. January 18, 2006. Accessed November 02, 2018. www.ynetnews.com/articles/0,7340,L-3202007,00.html.

[71] Cook, Jonathan. *Israel and the Clash of Civilizations Iraq, Iran and the Plan to Remake the Middle East.* London: Pluto Press, 2008.

[72] Goodrich, Thomas. *Hellstorm: The Death of Nazi Germany, 1944-1947.* Aberdeen Books, 2010.

[73] Ibid.

[74] Ibid.

[75] Ibid.

[76] Ibid.

77 Ibid.

78 Ibid.

79 Ibid.

80 Ibid.

81 Ibid.

82 Ibid.

83 Ibid.

84 Ibid.

85 'Archives Reveal Allies Feared Nazi Guerrilla War in Alps.' *The Local*, 29 Oct. 2010. www.thelocal.de/20101029/30831.

86 "Firebombing of Tokyo." *History.com*, A&E Television Networks. www.history.com/this-day-in-history/firebombing-of-tokyo.

87 Goldman, David P. *How Civilizations Die: (And Why Islam Is Dying Too)*. Washington, D.C.: Regnery Pub., 2011.

88 'The Avalon Project : Hamas Covenant 1988.' Avalon Project - Documents in Law, History and Diplomacy. Accessed July 20, 2018. http://avalon.law.yale.edu/20th_century/hamas.asp.

89 Pardo, Eldad. *Palestinian Elementary School Curriculum 2016–17: Radicalization and Revival of the PLO Program.* Hebrew University of Jerusalem. April 2017. Accessed July 22, 2018.

www.impact-se.org/wp-content/uploads/PA-Curriculum-20
17-Revised.pdf.

90 Ibid.

91 Ibid.

92 Yousafzai, Malala, and Christina Lamb. *I Am Malala: The Girl Who Stood up for Education and Was Shot by the Taliban*. UK: Weidenfeld & Nicolson, 2013.

93 'Palestinian Children's TV Teaches Terrorism, Anti-Semitism.' YouTube video, 6:38. 'Rebel Media,' September 28, 2015. www.youtube.com/watch?v=KXcQ892cKso.

94 'Qassam Rocket.' *Wikipedia*, Wikimedia Foundation, 13 July 2018. en.wikipedia.org/wiki/Qassam_rocket.

95 Al-Atrush, Samer. 'Gaza's Burning Kites and Explosives Strapped to Condoms Raise Tensions with Israel.' *The Telegraph*, Telegraph Media Group, 23 June 2018. www.telegraph.co.uk/news/2018/06/23/gazas-burning-kites -explosives-strapped-condoms-raise-tensions/.

96 'Population Transfer.' *Wikipedia*, Wikimedia Foundation, 14 July 2018. en.wikipedia.org/wiki/Population_transfer.

97 'Pied-Noir.' *Wikipedia*, Wikimedia Foundation, 18 July 2018. en.wikipedia.org/wiki/Pied-Noir.

98 Hill, Todd. '10 Notable Forced Migrations in Human History.' *Listosaur | Hungry for Knowledge*, 25 Aug. 2015. listosaur.com/history/10-notable-forced-migrations-in-hum an-history/.

99 Landau, Noa. 'UN Council: Israel Intentionally Shot Children and Journalists in Gaza.' *Haaretz*. February 28,

2019. Accessed June 13, 2019.
www.haaretz.com/israel-news/un-council-israel-intentional
ly-shot-children-and-journalists-in-gaza-1.6979358.

[100] 'Qatar.' Wikipedia. June 18, 2019. Accessed June 20, 2019. https://en.wikipedia.org/wiki/Qatar.

[101] 'Treatment and Rights in Arab Host States (Right to Return - Human Rights Watch Policy Page).' Human Rights Watch. Accessed July 26, 2018. www.hrw.org/legacy/campaigns/israel/return/arab-rtr.htm.

[102] Rosen, Steven J. 'Kuwait Expels Thousands of Palestinians.' *Middle East Quarterly* 19 (September 2012). September 2012. Accessed July 27, 2018. www.meforum.org/articles/2012/kuwait-expels-thousands-of-palestinians.

[103] Reuters. 'Libya Ousts And Strands Palestinians.' The New York Times. September 12, 1995. Accessed July 26, 2018. www.nytimes.com/1995/09/12/world/libya-ousts-and-stran ds-palestinians.html.

[104] Rosen, Steven J. 'Kuwait Expels Thousands of Palestinians.' *Middle East Quarterly.* 19 (September 2012). September 2012. Accessed July 27, 2018. www.meforum.org/articles/2012/kuwait-expels-thousands-of-palestinians.

[105] Ibid.

[106] Niv, Kobi. 'Has Our Expiration Date Arrived?' *Haaretz.* January 10, 2018. www.haaretz.com/opinion/.premium-has-our-expiration-da te-arrived-1.5177965.

[107] Pardo, Eldad. *Palestinian Elementary School Curriculum 2016–17: Radicalization and Revival of the PLO Program.* Hebrew University of Jerusalem. April 2017. Accessed July 22, 2018.

[108] Weaver, Matthew. '12 Camels Disqualified from Saudi Beauty Contest in 'Botox' Row.' *The Guardian.* January 24, 2018. Accessed September 20, 2018. www.theguardian.com/world/2018/jan/24/saudi-camel-beauty-contest-judges-get--hump-botox-cheats.

[109] Harris, Sam. *The End of Faith: Religion, Terror, and the Future of Reason.* New York: W.W. Norton, 2005.

[110] Burke, Edmund. *Reflections on the Revolution in France.* 2016, in the version translated by Jonathan Bennett presented at www.earlymoderntexts.com

[111] 'French Workers Get "Right to Disconnect" from Emails out of Hours.' BBC News. December 31, 2016. Accessed June 24, 2019. www.bbc.com/news/world-europe-38479439.

[112] Bregman, Rutger. *Utopia for Realists: The Case for a Universal Basic Income, Open Borders, and a 15-hour Workweek.* Amsterdam: Correspondent, 2016.

[113] Patai, Raphael. *The Arab Mind.* Tucson, AZ: Recovery Resources Press, 2014.

[114] '1948 Arab–Israeli War.' Wikipedia. September 14, 2018. Accessed September 21, 2018. https://en.wikipedia.org/wiki/1948_Arab–Israeli_War.

[115] 'حلقات النكبة الفلسطينية ـ الجزء الثالث ـ محمد إلهامي مع محمد ناصر.' YouTube video, 1:13:41. 'محمد إلهامي,' May 20, 2017. www.youtube.com/watch?v=Ckl5_wxqXDk.

116 Kurtzman, Daniel. 'Hilarious Quotes from Baghdad Bob.' ThoughtCo. Accessed September 21, 2018. www.thoughtco.com/baghdad-bob-quotes-4068522.

117 Savyon, A., and Yigal Carmon. 'The Iran-U.S. Crisis Following Soleimani's Killing – Analysis And Assessment: Part I.' MEMRI. Middle East Media Research Institute, January 6, 2020. www.memri.org/reports/iran-us-crisis-following-soleimanis-killing---analysis-and-assessment-part-i.

118 Oren, Michael. 'The Coming Middle East Conflagration.' The Atlantic. Atlantic Media Company, November 5, 2019. www.theatlantic.com/ideas/archive/2019/11/israel-preparing-open-war/601285/.

119 'Turkish Contestant Fails to Answer "Where Is Great Wall of China?"' Hürriyet Daily News. August 06, 2018. Accessed August 07, 2018. www.hurriyetdailynews.com/turkish-contestant-fails-to-answer-where-is-great-wall-of-china-135495.

120 Gearing, Jes. 'A Note on Arabic Literacy and Translation.' *Beyond Words - Language Blog*, August 10, 2009. Accessed July 24, 2018. www.altalang.com/beyond-words/a-note-on-arabic-literacy-and-translation/.

121 Harris, Sam. *The End of Faith: Religion, Terror, and the Future of Reason*. New York: W.W. Norton &, 2005.

122 Gearing, Jes. 'A Note on Arabic Literacy and Translation.' *Beyond Words - Language Blog,* August 10, 2009. Accessed July 24, 2018.

www.altalang.com/beyond-words/a-note-on-arabic-literacy
-and-translation/.

123 Akyol, Mustafa. 'Bolshevism in a Headdress.' The
American Enterprise Institute, April 1, 2005.
www.aei.org/articles/bolshevism-in-a-headdress/.

124 Reilly, Robert R. *The Closing of the Muslim Mind: How
Intellectual Suicide Created the Modern Islamist Crisis*.
Wilmington, DE: ISI Books, 2015.

125 Glubb, John. *The Fate of Empires and Search for
Survival*. Edinburgh: Blackwood, 1978.

126 Overbye, Dennis. 'How Islam Won, and Lost, the Lead in
Science.' *The New York Times*, 30 Oct. 2001.
www.nytimes.com/2001/10/30/science/how-islam-won-and
-lost-the-lead-in-science.html.

127 'The Intellectual Collapse of Islam.' YouTube video,
10:18. 'ThePoliticalBrain,' April 14, 2012.
www.youtube.com/watch?v=Fl1nJC3lvFs.

128 Reilly, Robert R. *The Closing of the Muslim Mind: How
Intellectual Suicide Created the Modern Islamist Crisis*.
Wilmington, DE: ISI Books, 2015.

129 Reilly, Robert R. *The Closing of the Muslim Mind: How
Intellectual Suicide Created the Modern Islamist Crisis*.
Wilmington, DE: ISI Books, 2015.

130 'The Atlas of Creation.' Wikipedia. July 17, 2018.
Accessed July 23, 2018.
https://en.wikipedia.org/wiki/The_Atlas_of_Creation.

131 'Ex-Muslim Atheist Making Stupid Zakir Naik Angry on
Evolution.' YouTube video, 7:59. 'Singhmanvir025,'

December 12, 2015.
www.youtube.com/watch?v=O7yKiAbM5MY.

132 Khaldūn, Ibn. *The Muqaddimah: an Introduction to History*. Princeton: Princeton University Press, 2015.

133 Zorba, Serkan. 'Muslims and Their Chronic Intellectual Stagnation.' IslamiCity. Accessed July 25, 2018. www.islamicity.org/6318/muslims-and-their-chronic-intellectual-stagnation/.

134 Hameed, Salman. 'Muslim Thought on Evolution Takes a Step Forward.' *The Guardian*. January 11, 2013. Accessed July 25, 2018. www.theguardian.com/commentisfree/belief/2013/jan/11/muslim-thought-on-evolution-debate.

135 Voltaire. *Treatise on Tolerance*. 2018, in the version tranlsated by Jonathan Bennett presented at www.earlymoderntexts.com

136 Quṭb, Sayyid. *Milestones*. Birmingham: Maktabah Booksellers and Publishers, 2006.

137 Harris, Sam, and Maajid Nawaz. *Islam and the Future of Tolerance a Dialogue*. Cambridge, MA: Harvard University Press, 2015.

138 Hatina, Meir. *Identity Politics in the Middle East: Liberal Thought and Islamic Challenge in Egypt*. London: Tauris Academic Studies, 2007.

139 'Egyptian Medical Doctor Criticizes the Phenomenon of Accepting Unscientific Islamic Beliefs, like the Notion That a Woman's Pregnancy Can Last Up to Four Years.' MEMRI. January 03, 2010. Accessed July 24, 2018. www.memri.org/reports/egyptian-medical-doctor-criticizes

-phenomenon-accepting-unscientific-islamic-beliefs-notion
.

[140] Brown, Jonathan A. C. *Misquoting Muhammad: The Challenge and Choices of Interpreting the Prophets Legacy.* London: Oneworld, 2014.

[141] Plato. *Six Great Dialogues: Apology, Crito, Phaedo, Phaedrus, Symposium, the Republic.* Mineola, NY: Dover, 2007.

[142] 'Middle East | Breastfeeding Fatwa Causes Stir.' BBC News. May 22, 2007. http://news.bbc.co.uk/2/hi/middle_east/6681511.stm.

[143] Brown, Jonathan A. C. *Misquoting Muhammad: The Challenge and Choices of Interpreting the Prophets Legacy.* London: Oneworld, 2014.

[144] Ibid.

[145] Ibid.

[146] Weaver, Richard M. *Ideas Have Consequences.* Chicago: University of Chicago Press, 2013.

[147] Junger, Sebastian. *Tribe: On Homecoming and Belonging.* New York: Twelve, 2016.

[148] Hobbes, Thomas. *Leviathan.* 2006, in the version translated by Jonathan Bennett presented at www.earlymoderntexts.com

[149] Reilly, Robert R. *The Closing of the Muslim Mind: How Intellectual Suicide Created the Modern Islamist Crisis.* Wilmington, DE: ISI Books, 2015.

150 Brown, Jonathan A. C. *Misquoting Muhammad: The Challenge and Choices of Interpreting the Prophets Legacy.* London: Oneworld, 2014.

151 Wax, Emily. 'Islam Attracting Many Survivors of Rwanda Genocide.' *The Washington Post.* September 23, 2002. Accessed October 05, 2018. www.washingtonpost.com/wp-dyn/articles/A53018-2002Sep22.html?noredirect=on.

152 Voltaire. *Treatise on Tolerance.* 2018, in the version translated by Jonathan Bennett presented at www.earlymoderntexts.com

153 Rousseau, Jean-Jacques. *The Social Contract.* 2010, in the version translated by Jonathan Bennett presented at www.earlymoderntexts.com

154 Ramadan, Tariq. *What I Believe.* Oxford: Oxford University Press, 2010.

155 Akyol, Mustafa. *Islam without Extremes: a Muslim Case for Liberty.* New York: W.W. Norton & Company, 2013.

156 'Q&A with Sherif Gaber.' YouTube video, 30:01. 'Sherif Gaber,' October 09, 2017. www.youtube.com/watch?v=ThG4dzJyuT8.

157 Ay, Jallow. 'Freedom of Expression from the Islamic Perspective.' *Journal of Mass Communication & Journalism* 5, no. 10 (October 29, 2015). Accessed July 31, 2018. doi:10.4172/2165-7912.1000278.

158 Akyol, Mustafa. 'Is Free Speech Good for Muslims?' *The New York Times.* March 27, 2017. Accessed July 30, 2018.

www.nytimes.com/2017/03/27/opinion/is-free-speech-good -for-muslims.html.

159 Bergesen, Albert James. 'A Durkheimian Theory of "Witch-Hunts" with the Chinese Cultural Revolution of 1966-1969 as an Example.' *Journal for the Scientific Study of Religion* 17, no. 1 (March 1978): 19-29. doi:10.2307/1385424.

160 Hollingsworth, Julia. 'Christchurch Terror Attack Death Toll Increases to 51.' CNN. May 02, 2019. Accessed June 11, 2019. https://edition.cnn.com/2019/05/02/asia/nz-christchurch-att ack-death-toll-intl/index.html.

161 Harris, Sam. *The End of Faith: Religion, Terror, and the Future of Reason.* New York: W.W. Norton, 2005.

162 Esposito, John L. *The Future of Islam.* New York, NY: Oxford University Press, 2013.

163 Harari, Yuval Noah. *21 Lessons for the 21st Century.* London: Jonathan Cape, 2018.

164 'Messiah Mode [FULL].' YouTube video, 1:26:59. 'David Sheen,' February 6, 2020. www.youtube.com/watch?v=eFl4U2NRJTg.

165 Cummins, Will. 'Muslims Are a Threat to Our Way of Life.' *The Telegraph.* July 25, 2004. Accessed June 25, 2019. www.telegraph.co.uk/comment/personal-view/3608849/Mu slims-are-a-threat-to-our-way-of-life.html.

166 Cummins, Will. 'The Tories Must Confront Islam Instead of Kowtowing to It.' *The Telegraph.* July 18, 2004. Accessed July 01, 2019. www.telegraph.co.uk/comment/personal-view/3608563/Th

e-Tories-must-confront-Islam-instead-of-kowtowing-to-it.h
tml.

167 Abruzzo, Shavana. 'New Yorkistan? Don't Rule It Out!'
New York Post. June 22, 2010. Accessed July 01, 2019.
https://nypost.com/2010/06/22/new-yorkistan-dont-rule-it-o
ut/.

168 Esposito, John L. *What Everyone Needs to Know about
Islam (2nd Edition)*. Oxford University Press, USA, 2011.

169 Kurtz, Howard. 'National Review Cans Columnist Ann
Coulter.' *The Washington Post*. October 02, 2001. Accessed
July 01, 2019.
www.washingtonpost.com/archive/lifestyle/2001/10/02/nati
onal-review-cans-columnist-ann-coulter/4128f3be-7a64-47
e9-a350-eb801757d376/?utm_term=.97382bd5495d.

170 Esposito, John L. *The Future of Islam*. New York, NY:
Oxford University Press, 2013.

171 Lean, Nathan. 'Richard Dawkins Does It Again: New
Atheism's Islamophobia Problem.' Salon. August 10, 2013.
Accessed June 25, 2019.
www.salon.com/2013/08/10/richard_dawkins_does_it_agai
n_new_atheisms_islamophobia_problem/.

172 Bienkov, Adam. 'Boris Johnson Wrote That "Islam Is the
Problem" and Defended Islamophobia as a "Natural
Reaction."' *Business Insider*. August 06, 2018. Accessed
June 25, 2019.
www.businessinsider.com/boris-johnson-islam-is-the-probl
em-and-islamophobia-is-a-natural-reaction-2018-8.

173 Hasan, Mehdi. 'Douglas Murray, the EDL, Dodgy
Videos and Me.' HUFFPOST. July 30, 2013. Accessed June

25, 2019.
www.huffingtonpost.co.uk/mehdi-hasan/douglas-murray-e
dl-dodgy-videos-me_b_3675193.html?guccounter=1&guce
_referrer=aHR0cHM6Ly93d3cuZ29vZ2xlLmNvbS8&guce
_referrer_sig=AQAAAFS2N_zA2QDaKJsFBqQdRYdvr9h
eObUuRkT3OLaD11odS0gNDv_X8bNqZIiP2w-p3RFwvc
-Vk57EThI2jEt_nS9_745UoeS4tKhahGo7nHO2kPPrWqQ
1mNIlg4Z__SY1y2Elwm7w285NJaPCx6ojhjkQYlzrLzTq
qdz3_HaRmdFz.

[174] Topping, Alexandra. 'Katie Hopkins Leaves LBC Radio Show after "Final Solution" Tweet.' *The Guardian*. May 26, 2017. Accessed June 25, 2019. www.theguardian.com/media/2017/may/26/katie-hopkins-l eaves-lbc-radio-final-solution-tweet-manchester-attack.

[175] Akyol, Mustafa. *Islam without Extremes: a Muslim Case for Liberty*. New York: W.W. Norton & Company, 2013.

[176] Mirkinson, Jack. '*Newsweek's* "MUSLIM RAGE" Cover Draws Angry Protest.' The Huffington Post. December 07, 2017. Accessed July 31, 2018. www.huffingtonpost.com/2012/09/17/newsweek-muslim-ra ge-cover_n_1890124.html.

[177] Dalrymple, Theodore. *Spoilt Rotten: The Toxic Cult of Sentimentality*. London: Gibson Square, 2017.

[178] Ibid.

[179] Ibid.

[180] Ibid.

[181] Harris, Sam, and Maajid Nawaz. *Islam and the Future of Tolerance a Dialogue*. Cambridge, MA: Harvard University Press, 2015.

182 Gerecht, Reuel Marc. 'A Muslim Identity Crisis.' *The Weekly Standard.* September 05, 2014. Accessed June 25, 2019. www.weeklystandard.com/reuel-marc-gerecht/a-muslim-identity-crisis.

183 Karasz, Palko. '85,000 Children in Yemen May Have Died of Starvation.' *The New York Times.* November 21, 2018. Accessed January 30, 2019. www.nytimes.com/2018/11/21/world/middleeast/yemen-famine-children.html.

184 'Dozens of Children Killed in Saudi-led Airstrike on Bus - CNN Video.' CNN. August 10, 2018. Accessed January 30, 2019. https://edition.cnn.com/videos/world/2018/08/09/yemen-children-bus-attack-pkg-elbagir-vpx.cnn.

185 Cecil, Nicholas. 'Missing Saudi Journalist "Cut up with Bone Saw in Pulp Fiction Murder."' *Evening Standard.* October 10, 2018. Accessed October 29, 2018. https://www.standard.co.uk/news/world/jamal-khashoggi-saudi-journalist-cut-up-with-bone-saw-in-pulp-fiction-murder-inside-consulate-in-a3958256.html.

186 Peterson, Jordan B. *12 Rules for Life: An Antidote for Chaos.* London: Allen Lane, 2018.

187 Voltaire. *Treatise on Tolerance.* 2018, in the version translated by Jonathan Bennett presented at www.earlymoderntexts.com

188 Solzhenitsyn, Aleksandr Isaevich. *The Gulag Archipelago.* London: Vintage Classics, 2018.

189 Hobbes, Thomas. *Leviathan*. 2006, in the version translated by Jonathan Bennett presented at www.earlymoderntexts.com

190 'Last Sermon of the Prophet Muhammad (PBUH).' Facts About the Muslims & the Religion of Islam. Accessed August 02, 2018. www.whyislam.org/muhammad/last-sermon-of-the-prophet -muhammad-pbuh/.

191 Glubb, John. *The Fate of Empires and Search for Survival*. Edinburgh: Blackwood, 1978.

192 Oruç, Merve Şebnem. 'It Is Our History, Idiot.' *DailySabah*. December 10, 2014. Accessed August 01, 2019. www.dailysabah.com/columns/merve-sebnem-oruc/2014/1 2/10/it-is-our-history-idiot.

193 İnönü, İsmet. *Hatıralar*. İstanbul: Bilgi, 1988.

194 Akyol, Mustafa. *Islam without Extremes: a Muslim Case for Liberty*. New York: W.W. Norton & Company, 2013.

195 Farole, Safia. 'Race Matters: Colorblind Racism in the Ummah.' Muslimmatters. February 21, 2011. Accessed August 02, 2018. https://muslimmatters.org/2011/02/21/race-matters-colorbli nd-racism-in-the-ummah/.

196 Dolsten, Josefin. '18 Jewish Groups Urge Congress to Pass Bill to End Trump's Travel Ban.' Jewish Telegraphic Agency. April 11, 2019. Accessed August 01, 2019. www.jta.org/quick-reads/18-jewish-groups-urge-congress-t o-pass-bill-to-end-trumps-muslim-travel-ban.

197 Meotti, Giulio. 'Chanting "Jews, Remember Khaybar" in Italy.' Israel National News. January 01, 2018. Accessed

August 01, 2019.
www.israelnationalnews.com/Articles/Article.aspx/21495.

[198] Ali, Ayaan Hirsi. *Infidel*. New York: Atria Paperback, 2013.

[199] Ali, Ayaan Hirsi. *Heretic: Why Islam Needs a Reformation Now*. New York: HarperCollins US, 2015.

[200] Harris, Sam. *The End of Faith: Religion, Terror, and the Future of Reason*. New York: W.W. Norton, 2005.

[201] Harris, Sam, and Maajid Nawaz. *Islam and the Future of Tolerance a Dialogue*. Cambridge, MA: Harvard University Press, 2015.

[202] Nydell, Margaret K. *Understanding Arabs: A Contemporary Guide to Arab Society*. Boston: Intercultural Press, an Imprint of Nicholas Brealey Publishing, 2014.

[203] Aslan, Reza. *No God but God: The Origins and Evolution of Islam*. New York: Ember, 2012.

[204] Ibid.

[205] Brown, Jonathan A. C. *Misquoting Muhammad: The Challenge and Choices of Interpreting the Prophets Legacy*. London: Oneworld, 2014.

[206] 'Fatima Al-Fihri.' Wikipedia. Wikimedia Foundation. September 9, 2019. https://en.wikipedia.org/wiki/Fatima_al-Fihri.

[207] Montagu, Mary Wortley. *The Turkish Embassy Letters*. London: Virago, 2009.

208 Brown, Jonathan A. C. *Misquoting Muhammad: The Challenge and Choices of Interpreting the Prophets Legacy.* London: Oneworld, 2014.

209 Nydell, Margaret K. *Understanding Arabs: A Contemporary Guide to Arab Society.* Boston: Intercultural Press, an Imprint of Nicholas Brealey Publishing, 2014.

210 Ibid.

211 Ibid.

212 'BBC Documentary - Teen Model Factory of Russia.' YouTube video, 55:59. 'Amazing Documentaries,' November 19, 2016. www.youtube.com/watch?v=GE-ZDS86F9k.

213 Nydell, Margaret K. *Understanding Arabs: A Contemporary Guide to Arab Society.* Boston: Intercultural Press, an Imprint of Nicholas Brealey Publishing, 2014.

214 Junger, Sebastian. *Tribe: On Homecoming and Belonging.* New York: Twelve, 2016.

215 Jones, E. Michael. *Libido Dominandi: Sexual Liberation and Political Control.* South Bend, IN: St. Augustines Press, 2005.

216 Fortuna, Roger, and Suzan Clarke. 'For Women Who Want Kids, "The Sooner the Better": 90 Percent of Eggs Gone By Age 30.' ABC News. January 29, 2010. https://abcnews.go.com/GMA/OnCall/women-fertility-falls-lose-90-percent-eggs-30/story?id=9693015.

217 Smith, Helen. *Men on Strike: Why Men Are Boycotting Marriage, Fatherhood, and the American Dream—And Why It Matters.* New York: Encounter Books, 2015.

218 'Brain Chemistry May Hold Clues to Women's Stress.' Latest Yorkshire News, June 15, 2010. www.yorkshirepost.co.uk/news/latest-news/brain-chemistry-may-hold-clues-to-women-s-stress-1-2577821.

219 Goldman, David P. *How Civilizations Die: (And Why Islam Is Dying Too)*. Washington, D.C.: Regnery Pub., 2011.

220 Qutb, Sayyid. *The America I Have Seen*. Kashf ul Shubuhat Publications, 1951. Accessed October 27, 2018. www.cia.gov/library/abbottabad-compound/3F/3F56ACA473044436B4C1740F65D5C3B6_Sayyid_Qutb_-_The_America_I_Have_Seen.pdf.

221 Ibid.

222 Ibid.

223 'Statue of Turkey's First Ballerina Damaged in Sexual Assault.' *Hürriyet Daily News*. November 20, 2018. Accessed January 30, 2019. www.hurriyetdailynews.com/statue-of-turkeys-first-ballerina-damaged-in-sexual-assault-139015.

224 Weisman, Carrie. 'Why Porn Is Exploding in the Middle East.' Salon. January 22, 2015. Accessed August 28, 2018. www.salon.com/2015/01/15/why_porn_is_exploding_in_the_middle_east_partner/.

225 Patai, Raphael. *The Arab Mind*. Tucson, AZ: Recovery Resources Press, 2014.

226 Pipes, Daniel. *In the Path of God: Islam and Political Power*. Routledge, 2017.

227 Rousseau, Jean-Jacques. *The Social Contract*. 2010, in the version translated by Jonathan Bennett presented at www.earlymoderntexts.com

228 Stewart, Emily. 'Trump Says China's Xi Is "President for Life" - and Maybe America Should Try It.' Vox. March 04, 2018. Accessed June 10, 2019. www.vox.com/policy-and-politics/2018/3/4/17077642/trump-xi-china-fundraiser.

229 Rousseau, Jean-Jacques. *The Social Contract*. 2010, in the version by Jonathan Bennett presented at www.earlymoderntexts.com

230 Tocqueville, Alexis De. *DEMOCRACY IN AMERICA*. LONDON ENGLAND: PENGUIN Books, 2003.

231 Hoffer, Eric. *The Ordeal of Change*. Titusville, NJ: Hopewell Publications, 2006.

232 Akyol, Mustafa. *Islam without Extremes: a Muslim Case for Liberty*. New York: W.W. Norton & Company, 2013.

233 Harari, Yuval Noah. *21 Lessons for the 21st Century*. London: Jonathan Cape, 2018.

234 Hoffer, Eric. *The Ordeal of Change*. Titusville, NJ: Hopewell Publications, 2006.

235 Ibid.

236 Bon, Gustave Le. *The Crowd: a Study of the Popular Mind*. Mineola, NY: Dover Publications, 2002.

237 Bregman, Rutger. *Utopia for Realists: The Case for a Universal Basic Income, Open Borders, and a 15-hour Workweek*. Amsterdam: Correspondent, 2016.

[238] Junger, Sebastian. *Tribe: On Homecoming and Belonging*. New York: Twelve, 2016.

[239] Burke, Edmund. *Reflections on the Revolution in France*. 2016, in the version translated by Jonathan Bennett presented at www.earlymoderntexts.com

[240] De Montaigne, Michel. *Essays, Book I*. 2017, in the version tranlsated by Jonathan Bennett presented at www.earlymoderntexts.com